Eat Well For Less

Happy & Healthy

BBC Books, an imprint of Ebury Publishing
20 Vauxhall Bridge Road,
London SW1V 2SA

BBC Books is part of the Penguin Random House group of companie
addresses can be found at global.penguinrandomhouse.com

This book is published to accompany the television series entitled *Eat Well for Less?*
first broadcast on BBC One in 2015.

Commissioning Editor: Ricky Cooper and Nasfim Haque
Executive Producer: Jo Scarratt-Jones
Series Producer: Fiona Gay

First published by BBC Books in 2022

www.penguin.co.uk

A CIP catalogue record for this book is available from the British Library

ISBN 9781785947841

Project Editor: Nell Warner
Contributing Writer: Sally Somers
Design: maru studio
Food photography: Andrew Burton
Home Economist and Food Stylist: Janet Brinkworth
Assistant Home Economists: David Birt and Chris Start

Additional photography: p.14 calum-lewis/Unsplash; p.30 fotofabrika/Adobe stock;
p.32–33 Tatiana Atamaniuk/Adobe stock; p.36–37 photka/Adobe stock

Printed and bound by Firmengruppe APPL, aprinta druck, Wemding, Germany

Penguin Random House is committed to a sustainable future
for our business, our readers and our planet. This book is made
from Forest Stewardship Council® certified paper.

Eat Well
For Less

Happy & Healthy

Jo Scarratt-Jones

FOREWORD BY **Chris Bavin** AND **Jordan Banjo**

BOOKS

Contents

Forewords

Hello, Chris here! I've been doing *Eat Well For Less* for eight years now, and some things do change – like my new co-presenter Jordan! – but lots remain the same... I still hear that cooking is complicated and time consuming and eating healthy is expensive. I promise you, it really isn't, and the fact that you're reading this gives me hope that you believe it doesn't need to be! This book is full of tips and tricks that will make things easier and enjoyable in the kitchen. You can hold me to that!

I know just how *Eat Well For Less* has not only helped the families we film with, but also those who watch the series. I love hearing your stories, especially when we are living through a period when food is hitting the headlines more than usual, with interruptions to the supply chain, shortages, price increases, food banks and of course the ethical or environmental impact on our planet. I feel very proud to be part of something that is helping us all.

If I could only give you one bit of advice – and let's face it, I have lots I could tell you! – it would be to PLAN. Now, I know that can sound really dull and boring, but honestly a bit of meal planning can make all the difference – keeping a list of foods that you actually need and don't already have lurking at the back of your cupboard, which will not only mean less stress when you're cooking but will make sure that you're not spending when you don't need to. And of course less waste. Try it, you'll be surprised at how, just by spending a little bit of time planning your food week, it will actually result in more time for you! Happy cooking!

Hello, Jordan here, the newbie! Thank you for watching the series – and reading this book! It's great to be part of the *Eat Well For Less* family. I've always been a fan of the show and now to be part of it is so exciting and I've learnt so much along the way. Like a lot of us, I'm always busy, and with two young children I was definitely one those people who was grabbing food on the go and relying on convenience shopping, but actually making this series has made me look at my own habits and made me a lot more aware of my choices. All for the better!

As well as delicious recipes, you'll see we've got lots of info-packed sections, from how to get kitchen confident to working with store cupboard ingredients, saving time and wasting less, cooking for all tastes, and my favourite – eating healthy breakfasts and lunches on the go! There really is something for everyone.

I know some of you may not be confident cooks, and some of you will think you don't have the time, but honestly, if I can find a way to make these recipes work, anyone can! Go on, give them a whirl!

Chris & Jordan

Feeling at home
in the kitchen

When someone says, 'I don't like cooking', what they are often saying is they think they are no good at it. Because who enjoys doing something they can't do? It's no wonder cooking can seem like a thankless, and often daunting, task – feeling deflated when all your efforts have been met with thumbs-down is no one's idea of fun. But once you pull off a simple dish that delivers happy faces and clean plates all round, that negative cycle turns into a positive one. And a simple dish is all it takes to start that journey: you see your skills increase and your confidence flourish, and the kitchen soon becomes your happy place.

Clearing the decks

Have a two-minute whip around the worktops before you start cooking, and you'll thank yourself later. That stack of paperwork by the kettle? Move it somewhere else. Put kitchen utensils back in their place to avoid any frantic rummaging while you are stirring the pot. Tidy away anything that you won't be needing, and create a clear space on which to work. Then it's just a matter of wiping down the surfaces and you are good to go.

Small spaces
Lack of space doesn't mean you can't produce fantastic food, and some of the best-tasting food comes out of tiny street stalls. Clearing up as you go rather than letting it all build up into one mighty pile is key, as is maximising the space you do have. If there's a gadget you rarely use, store it away in a cupboard. Prioritise space for the things you use often. The good news is that the smaller the kitchen, the quicker it is to tidy...

Finding the recipe for you

It might seem obvious, but finding your own cooking level is key: pace yourself if you are starting out or not feeling that confident. The recipes in this book are all easy to follow, use everyday ingredients and keep budgets in mind (and it goes without saying they are all delicious!), so use these as a launchpad, and – at least to start with – stick to the recipe.

Read the recipe!
You will often see the words 'read the recipe through before you start'. But why? Well, who hasn't got stuck in only to find halfway through that you hadn't noticed the oven timing or are missing a vital ingredient? A quick scan right through the recipe steps means you can avoid:
- Nipping out to the shops mid-cook for a missing ingredient...
- ... or having to make an ingredient or even whole dish switch, which will throw you off course and just add time and stress
- Any sudden surprises, like marinating or long cooking times you hadn't factored in

GETTING BACK INTO THE *GROOVE*

Maybe you are someone who used to enjoy cooking, but it's become a chore and a headache? Different dietary needs, picky eaters and lack of time and inspiration all take their toll on the family cook. In a quest to please everyone, reaching for ready meals and takeaways can feel like the only option – then, before you know it, they have become more than just an occasional treat, and the cost is stacking up. It's time to get that spring back in your step...

GLOSSARY
of
COOKING TERMS

Beat: stir rapidly to make a mixture smooth, using a whisk, spoon or food mixer.

Blanch: briefly plunge ingredients into boiling water, to seal in colour and flavour (before freezing or, in the case of tomatoes, to making peeling easier).

Blend: combine ingredients thoroughly until uniform, using a whisk or spoon, or a food mixer or blender.

Boil: heat a liquid until it is bubbling

Braise: cook by gently simmering in a small amount of liquid in a covered pan.

Cream: beat ingredients (usually butter and sugar, for example in a cake) together until combined and smooth.

Fold: spoon lighter ingredients (often whisked egg whites) into heavier ones, using a large metal spoon or rubber spatula in big, circular movements, to keep as much air in as possible.

Grease: lightly coat the insides of a baking tin with butter or oil, to prevent the finished dish or cake sticking.

Marinate: coat ingredients, usually meat or fish, in a sauce or paste so that the flavours are absorbed by the ingredient.

Par-boil: partially boil an ingredient, most often potatoes and root veg before roasting, to reduce final cooking time and maximise texture.

Poach: cook very gently in barely simmering liquid.

Purée: blend or mash ingredients until completely smooth – usually using a blender, food processor or sieve.

Reduce: thicken a liquid by boiling, resulting in a more concentrated and intense flavour.

Roast: cooking meat, poultry or veg, in the oven.

Rub in: break down the butter into a breadcrumb-like consistency by rubbing it into the flour using your fingertips.

Sauté: cook food in a frying pan in a little oil, moving it about to cook all sides evenly.

Simmer: cook food in liquid that is just below boiling, so bubbling gently.

Steam: cook food in a steamer or on a rack set over a small amount of boiling water in a covered pan, so the food cooks in the steam created.

Steep/soak: leave ingredients in hot or warm liquid to extract flavour and/or soften.

Stew: cook food in a sauce or liquid in a covered pan over a low heat on the stove or in the oven, usually for a few hours.

Stir-fry: fry food fairly briefly in a little oil over a high heat, stirring the ingredients constantly as they cook.

Toss: using two large spoons, or spoon and fork/salad tossers to turn ingredients very gently in order to combine any dressing etc.

Whisk: beat ingredients with a fork, hand whisk or whisk attachment on a food mixer, to blend and make uniform or to incorporate air.

All aboard!

Recruiting family members to the kitchen and getting them stuck in will bring multiple benefits. By involving everyone in the planning and cooking, you not only share the load but you turn the kitchen into a fun, creative space to hang out together. It's a fantastic way for children to learn and to take an interest in what they are eating, all while getting some great life skills and healthy habits under their belt. Children can pick things up pretty fast, and you may find you are all equals in the kitchen and can learn from each other. And, of course, their efforts and input mean they are more likely to give a thumbs-up to the results. What's more, when you are part of the process, you are more likely be nudged out of your comfort zone to try new things. It's a win-win-win!

As your confidence levels increase, you might even start taking turns to be in charge – a night off cooking no longer has to mean a takeaway. Share the responsibility and the work (including the clearing up!), and you can all share the pleasure too.

KITCHEN CHAT

More than just getting the whole family to help out, cooking together also gets you together in the same room – a great opportunity to talk about the day and generally hang out. We tend to all gravitate to different parts of the house to get on with our own stuff, but it's not for nothing the kitchen is referred to as the heart of the home. Cooking alongside each other is a natural conversation starter and provides a comfortable environment for opening up. You might find you get more chat out of your teenager over a chopped onion than you have all week!

Don't be afraid to ask

We aren't born knowing how to dice an onion, and there's no shame in looking for tips and help for even the simplest of cooking instructions. There are plenty of people out there who can offer advice – friends and family, or the internet is a treasure trove of hacks and visual guides. Even seasoned professionals expand their skills this way, so you're in good company.

Go with the flow

It's no surprise that the more you cook, the better you get and the more confident you get. You soon get into the swing of it, and find yourself turning out a dish without even having to focus too much on it. Then it's time to start adding your own touches and tweaks to a recipe, or to branch out into more adventurous or challenging dishes. Have faith in your instincts and what you think will taste good, and have fun playing with flavours and variations.

tips

FOR GETTING CHILDREN ON BOARD

1. **Share the legwork:** get everyone to find dishes they'd like to eat and/or cook – start with the recipes in this book, but the internet offers plenty of inspiration.

2. **Get them cooking their favourite dishes:** if they want to eat it, they are more likely to want to cook it.

3. **Offer a swap:** you help with homework, they help with the dinner.

4. **Encourage them to record their cooking success** on a phone or device, and to share it with select family and friends.

tips

FOR BROADENING YOUR HORIZONS

1. Don't assume that because you don't like something you never will. It might be a question of giving it different treatment – if you don't like kale, for example, try it whizzed into pesto (see page 121).

2. Make swaps: would sweet potato be good in place of squash in a recipe, or courgette in place of aubergine?

3. Recreate your favourite takeaways at home (and save a fortune!) – see page 144 for a healthier but delicious take on fish and chips, page 173 for chicken kebabs, or page 183 for a Thai-style curry.

4. If you come across a new dish or ingredient you really like while you are eating out, **find out what it is and how to cook it.**

5. Not all 'experiments' work out first time... but **don't give up!** Tweak it try and again.

Practice makes speed

We all know that doing something often and repeatedly makes us better and faster at it, and it's no different with cooking. We aren't looking for perfection here – we can leave that to chefs and restaurants – but getting up to speed on things like chopping veg will save time and soon make it second nature.

Stuck in that rut

There's nothing wrong with a rotating list of fail-safe, tried-and-tested dishes that everyone will eat, but it's easy to get stuck and for those dishes to start feeling a little bit, well... boring. Ring the changes and try new recipes to keep everyone interested – shifting out of your comfort zone from time to time has a positive knock-on effect, and will make you a more confident and versatile cook. New dishes bring new energy and appetites to the table, and they broaden everyone's tastes. Use the meal planners (see page 209) at the back of this book for inspiration. Or devise your own. Coming up with themes when planning the week's meals – around the world, maybe, where everyone picks a different cuisine for each night – will bring instant variety to the table.

USE-BY/BEST-BEFORE DATES

Understanding what these terms mean will cut down on food waste and allay any anxiety about what is still ok to eat and what needs chucking.

USE-BY

You will see this term on products that go off quickly, and it relates to food safety, so don't mess with these dates: the food is safe to eat up to and on the date given, but not after. It's important to follow the storage guidance given on the packaging, and you can freeze food before its use-by date (never after), but remember to use it as soon as you have defrosted it.

BEST-BEFORE

This term appears on frozen and tinned goods, and dried foods, and the label relates to quality rather than safety. This means that food is safe to eat after the date given but may not be at its best, in terms of flavour and texture.

For some people, fear of bacteria and contamination can be a real barrier to cooking from scratch and gaining confidence in the kitchen, but there are some simple procedures that will set your mind at rest and keep the nasties away:

- Wash your hands before and after handling food
- Wipe down the surfaces before you start and when you finish
- Wipe up any spillages as you go
- Use separate chopping boards for raw meat or fish
- Scrub chopping boards thoroughly after use
- Keep raw food chilled
- Don't keep opened cans, or packs of raw meat, dairy or fish in the fridge: decant into airtight containers
- Defrost foods overnight in the fridge

- Get to grips with use-by dates (see opposite) and check your fridge regularly
- Reheat food thoroughly, until piping hot right through
- Cook food properly – the recipe will guide you on testing for when something is done
- Leave leftovers to cool before covering and transferring them to the fridge
- Throw away anything you aren't sure is still safe to eat

CLEAN & SAFE

Saving time
& money

With busy lives, cooking from scratch can feel like an extra headache and a time commitment too far. But you really can rustle up delicious meals in the time it takes to find and heat a ready meal or place a takeaway order. And at a fraction of the cost. A lot of the recipes in this book call for just 10 minutes of prepping – in other words hands-on time – then the stove, oven or slow cooker takes over while you sit back and relax. All it takes is a little thinking ahead...

Meal planning

It can feel a bit boring to think ahead, but planning what you're going to eat through the week ahead takes all the pressure off and means your shopping can be super-efficient – and money-saving. No more throwing away wilting veg that never quite made it to the salad, or finding you are missing the very thing you need to complete a dish. There's nothing wrong with opening the fridge and wondering what to throw together for dinner, and it can often hit the spot – but it doesn't work for everyone, and can be impossible to sustain night after night (whatever weird and wonderful combinations you are up for trying...).

tips

FOR MEAL PLANNING

1. **Consider what you have going on** in the coming week and plan the really easy meals for the busier nights.

2. **Give everyone a say and factor in who is going to be out** or home late on any night, and who is going to be doing the cooking.

3. **Think about special dietary needs** (see page 24) and maybe a few meat-free days?

4. Write down all the ingredients you need for the week's dishes, then **make a shopping list.**

5. **Check the cupboards and fridge** and cross off anything on the list that you already have.

Get ahead
Having a plan for what you are going to eat each night, and knowing the ingredients are all waiting for you when you walk in the door, will keep you focused and make you less likely to switch plans or resort to more expensive options. Get everyone involved in making a meal plan (see page 12) and you can cruise through the week.

Savvy shopping

This is where the big savings come in. Planning your meals in advance means you won't be paying for food you don't need or won't use, and will avoid any missing ingredients you do need.

List it
Dashing to the supermarket with no list is a recipe for disaster, and often results in getting home with only half the stuff you need, and whole lot more you don't... so put the kettle on, sit down and write that list. Ideally in the order that your local supermarket is laid out in. That way you won't be backtracking around the store and getting distracted by offers for things you don't need.

Get online
This is a top way to stick to buying only the things on your list, and to keep a careful watch on your budget. A supermarket website will keep track of everything you have bought in the past, making repeat purchases quick and easy, and sometimes a bit too convenient! Make sure you don't fall in to the trap of repeating your last week's shop without checking what you actually need... You would be wise to run a quick check on price options rather than automatically click on

your usual, and to check any special offers, as all these change frequently.

Something to bear in mind is that delivery isn't free, you can't pay by cash and the delivery slot needs to work for your schedule. Also, watch out for unwanted substitutions when your item is not in stock, and not being able to pick and choose fruit and veg in the state of ripeness you are after does not suit everyone. But ordering online can be a time saver and – for those easily lured into impulse buying – a good way to make sure you buy only what you need.

Shopping apps

While good old-fashioned pen and paper work for many of us, there are some nifty phone apps out there that can ease the shopping process, from helping to create your list, sorting it by aisle and notifying you on use-by dates, to giving tips on storing and even finding recipes that match your shopping choices. In fact, they can take the strain of pretty much everything short of carrying the bags inside the house for you.

Not-so-special offers

Buy one get one free/half price is only special if you are actually going to use the bigger quantity. Otherwise, think carefully about how likely you are to use the extra, and have a good look at the use-by date. Be wary of changing your meal plan to fit around a bargain buy – it may end up costing you more and throwing your food planning off. That said, there are genuine bargains to be had – if an ingredient you are buying anyway is on offer, count yourself lucky, and maybe think about buying extra and doing a spot of freezing or batch cooking (see page 18).

Premium brands

Many of us feel wedded to our favourite brands and are convinced we couldn't switch to a cheaper brand, but as blind-tasting shows, often people can't tell much difference in the taste! Experiment with supermarket-own-brands and find the substitutes you are happy to make. You might be surprised to find there are cheaper brands you actually prefer, and the savings can really add up.

Incredible bulk

Buying in bulk is usually cheaper but doesn't fit with everyone's budgeting or storage space. But if there are products with a long shelf life that you know you will get through, it makes sense to stock up if you have the budget and space.

Pick your packaging

Items sold in individual packs or sachets are bound to work out more expensive than when sold in a large bag or box, so check the price per 100g (often on the supermarket shelf price label) and consider if you actually need the individual portions. Measuring out your own oats, for example, rather than using a sachet, takes a matter of seconds and there's less waste packaging to deal with too.

Where possible, go for loose fruit and veg rather than pre-packaged, so you can pick the amount you need and cut down on plastic packaging waste.

tips

FOR SHIPSHAPE SHOPPING

1. **Make a list.** Then remember to take it along with you...

2. **Avoid shopping when hungry or tired,** when you are more likely to make poor choices.

3. **Do the maths on 'special' offers and deals;** whip out your calculator if necessary.

4. **Shop online** if that fits better with your routine or schedule.

5. **Experiment with switching brands.**

6. **Buy in bulk** if you have space and budget.

7. **Avoid individually packaged items.**

8. **Shop around:** supermarkets aren't always the cheapest for everything.

9. **Buy fruit and veg in season.**

Waste not

The national figures for how much food in the UK is thrown away are eye-popping, and for the individual household that means a waste of money as well as food. Your shopping list is key here (see page 15), making sure you buy only what you need. Storing food properly once home (see page 28) and checking regularly for use-by dates (see page 12), can keep your waste and shopping bill down too.

Eat with the seasons

Food flown in or shipped from abroad will usually cost more due to transport and import costs, so it makes sense to stick to fruit and veg that's in season locally. It will also be at its best, having travelled shorter distances and been picked more recently and in peak condition. Make yourself familiar with what is in season when and bear it in mind when planning meals.

Pre-cut *vs* whole

Packs of fresh pre-cut veg or grated cheese are a fantastic helping hand if you have difficulty cutting or chopping, but they work out way more expensive and can result in more waste. Avoid these short-cuts if you don't need them, and get chopping. It takes hardly any time, and the more you do it, the faster you get!

'Get everyone involved in making a meal plan, and you can cruise through the week.'

Small is beautiful...

... and can be cheaper. If you are lucky enough to live somewhere with a fresh-produce market and high-street shops, and can fit daytime shopping into your schedule, you can save money on some goods. You can buy what you need loose, rather than as a pre-packaged amount, which gives you more control. So you only want three potatoes, or 100g beef mince? No problem. You are also more likely to be walking to high-street shops and markets, so will only buy what you can comfortably carry home – another plus.

Fruit and veg markets/greengrocers

This is where you will notice at a glance what is in season (it will be piled high and looking fabulous) and can check the price difference from other times of year. Because fresh produce is sold at peak freshness, it won't always last as long as from supermarkets, so beware of buying too much at once. If you are eyeing the bargain bowls of fruit or veg, consider if you'll be able to eat it all before it goes off, or if there are other things you can use them in – bananas past their best, for instance, to make banana bread or ice cream (see pages 199 and 206), or past-peak fruit will still be good in a smoothie.

Butchers and fishmongers

Your friendly butcher will offer plenty of the cheaper cuts, and will be happy to chop, mince, roll and slice, as well as give handy cooking tips. Buying the exact weight you need keeps the spending in check. Likewise, a fishmonger will portion off the size you want, and will often have bargain offcuts going cheap.

Refill and wholefood shops

Refill shops – where you take your own containers and buy the weight you choose of dry goods such as pasta, pulses and cereals – are cropping up on high streets. Always worth a look, as they can sometimes work out cheaper.

Love your leftovers

Even with careful meal planning, you are bound to have leftovers occasionally, but don't throw them away! Save yourself time and money by repurposing them.

• **If you think you can eat leftovers within a few days,** cover well once cooled and store in the fridge. Reheat thoroughly, and take special care when storing and reheating rice.

• **If you won't be able to eat leftovers within 2–3 days,** leave to cool then decant into a freezer container, label and date it and store in the freezer. You might want to keep a list – written or on your phone – of what you put in the freezer and how many it will feed. This saves rummaging through the drawers and you can see at a glance what you have lined up and ready to defrost.

• **You can also plan to have leftovers.** If eating the same for lunch the next day doesn't bother you, cook extra. It saves you cooking twice. Or freeze the extra portion for another day. Make more of one or two elements of a dish to combine with other things into a lunch the next day. Cold chicken or roast vegetables, for example, can form the basis of a healthy lunchbox (see page 41).

More veg less meat

Cutting out meat altogether isn't for everyone, but cutting down on portion size and upping the veg content in a dish is a great way to enjoy your meat while spending less. It can also create a healthier plate.

• **Phase it in.** Gradually reduce the meat portion size on your plate and you'll get used to it and not feel short-changed.

• **Plan at least one,** but possibly several, meat-free days a week.

• Focus on **veggie meals that are full of flavour,** colour and spice.

• Find dishes that **are bulked out with veg and other ingredients** – see our Teriyaki Beef Stir Fry on page 140, where we pack in the veg but the result is still deliciously meaty.

• When making a meat chilli, **double (or even treble) the bean quantity and reduce the mince.** That way, the dish stretches further and you won't even notice the difference in flavour.

• Meat curries and stews can be **bulked out with extra veg,** while losing none of their rich meatiness.

Cheaper cuts

Steak night doesn't have to mean fillet – cheaper cuts, like rump or skirt, will still hit the spot. When slow-cooking lamb or beef, go for the cheaper cuts; they might need a little extra cooking time, but the results will still be delicious, sometimes even better. Look beyond the usual meats, too – our Goat Curry on page 179 is as flavoursome as lamb but can be less expensive. Offal has fallen out of fashion and you might need some persuasion to give it a go, but it is super-lean, nutritious and inexpensive.

Batch cooking

With a bit of advance planning, you won't need to make a different dinner from scratch every night. Maybe a quiet time over the weekend to cook up batches of food for freezing works for you – without the pressing midweek timetable, it can be a relaxing way to cook. Plus it's a great opportunity to get the children involved, without that evening rush to get food on the table. To entice them into the kitchen and get them onside, suggest some baking – or maybe snacks for lunchboxes in the week ahead (see page 40) is another tick off the list.

If a weekend cook-a-thon isn't your thing, simply double, or treble, the dinner quantities one night and freeze the extra in portions – that way you only cook once. Don't forget to label the portions, and make a note somewhere of what you have ready to go, then all you have to do is defrost the right number of portions – in the fridge all day is ideal – and reheat for dinner.

Not all recipes are suited to batch cooking and freezing, but you'll find plenty that are, with reliable favourites among them. Generally speaking, stews and soups work best, but baked goods such as cakes and muffins work well.

tips

FOR LEFTOVERS

1. **Leftover cooked meat** is great in a salad or sandwich the next day, or add to the omelette or frittata on pages 51 and 98.

2. **Rice, pasta and other grains** can be chilled and used as a base for a salad.

3. **Tomato sauce** freezes brilliantly and can be used in loads of dishes, from pizza (see page 132) to pasta.

4. Take any **soup** you don't finish (see Leek and Potato on page 94) in a thermos to work or school the next day.

5. Excess **houmous** (see page 76) makes a handy on-the-go snack.

6. Chill uneaten **baked potatoes**, then cut into thick slices and fry or oven-bake in a little oil, for delicious skin-on chips.

Short on freezer space?

If you don't mind eating the same thing within a day or two, simply make more than you need, cover and chill in the fridge. It will still be an effort-free evening, and sitting down to a home-cooked meal you didn't just have to prepare always feels like a treat. Check if something is suitable for storing in the fridge or freezer – there are tips and guidance in the individual recipes in this book.

So what are the best things to batch cook and freeze? And the ones to skip?

YES

✓ **Stews, curries and pulses dishes** (see our Goat Curry, Lamb Tagine, Veg Chilli and Dahl on pages 179, 160, 110 and 138)

✓ **Bolognaise sauce** (useful for transforming into different dishes: bulk it out with canned beans and spice it up, and you have an instant chilli)

✓ **Soups** (see our Tomato and Bean and Leek and Potato Soup recipes on pages 86 and 94)

✓ **Muffins** (see page 58)

✓ **Stocks** – if you make your own chicken or veg stock, it's easier to make a big quantity

✓ **Bread** (see our Cheese and Onion Bread recipe on page 94) – in slices is a good idea (see tips, right)

✓ **Biscuits** (also freeze uncooked dough, ready to bake on a rainy day)

NO

✗ **Fried food** (it will go soggy)

✗ **Eggs and egg-based dishes** (freezing alters the texture)

✗ **Pasta and rice dishes** – ok to fridge some of these for next-day lunches, but avoid freezing

✗ **Salads and salad veg with a high water content**, such as lettuce, cucumber, tomato

tips

ON FREEZING

1. **Cool food to room temperature quickly**, then freeze immediately.

2. **Store food in the portion sizes you will need** and no bigger, so you don't have to defrost more than you need.

3. **Wrap and seal foods well** in freezer bags or freezerproof containers, to prevent the food coming into contact with air, which causes 'freezer burn'.

4. **Choose the right size of container** for the amount of food you are freezing, so you don't have half-empty containers clogging up your freezer space.

5. **When freezing liquids, leave a little headroom** beneath the lid to allow for the liquid to expand.

6. **If freezing bread, sliced works best**, so you can take out one at a time; place a layer of greaseproof paper between each slice to prevent them sticking together.

7. **Freeze stock in an ice-cube tray or cake tin** then, once frozen, tip into a freezer bag.

8. **Label it!** You'll be amazed at how easy it is to forget what something is, especially if it's a vegetarian or vegan version.

Previously frozen foods

For food safety reasons, it's important not refreeze food, but if the ingredient was frozen raw first time around, then you are ok to freeze it once cooked. So if you have some frozen mince, for example, it's fine to defrost it and turn it into a bolognaise sauce, then you can freeze the cooked bolognaise.

Cooking for all the family

If everyone loved and ate the same foods, then cooking for the whole family would be easy. But it's not just about picky eaters and a spread of ages. Tastes, dietary needs and choices, as well as allergies, can make the task of coming up with one dinner for everyone seem all but impossible. It can create a load of extra work, and inevitably ends up costing more too. So, how to cater for everyone at once without going crazy? Well, we have some ideas...

Eating together

Does your kitchen sometimes seem like a non-stop restaurant? Busy families with different timetables can struggle to fix a time to sit down together. And with small children, one parent (or both) getting home late means it's impractical to eat at the same time, and making sure the children are fed before the countdown to bedtime is rightly a priority. It can easily slide into quick-fix meals for them, then another quick-fix later, with healthy options taking the hit. With all the extra prep and clearing up, by the end of the evening you can often feel like you haven't escaped the kitchen at all. But there are ways to minimise the work involved:

SNACKING

When dinner feels a long way off, or when that afternoon slump strikes, our thoughts turn to a snack. The body is telling you it needs fuel, but before you reach for the pack of biscuits, take a moment to work out when your next meal is, and if a piece of fruit would tide you over nicely. Sitting down to the evening meal when you're a bit hungry means everyone is more likely to enjoy what they are eating, and be up for trying new things. Often the best-tasting and most enjoyable meals are the ones where everyone sits down with a proper appetite.

Do

- **See if there's room for compromise on timings:** push the children's eating time a little later, and bring the adults' one a little earlier maybe?

- **Consider which dishes are suited to reheating later**, so you only have to cook once.

- **Meet the children halfway:** which of their favourite dinners are you up for, in exchange for them trying yours?

- **Lay down a few rules:** if small children aren't the issue but you still struggle to get everyone around the table at once, then let everyone know what time dinner is, and that you expect them to be there on time. Ideally a little early, to lay the table...

Don't

- **Think in terms of 'children's food' and 'grown-up food':** there are plenty of recipes – especially in this book! – that the whole family will love.

- **Feel you have to eliminate certain dishes** because they are something aimed only at children: chicken nuggets are easily transformed into home-made goujons, for instance – healthier and more delicious for everyone.

- **Load children up with too many snacks** when delaying their meal (see left).

Cooking together

As soon as children are old enough to be given a job in the kitchen, get them involved. Turning meals into a family effort makes them a shared experience. At first, the 'help' might feel like it's adding more work for you, and is slowing you down, but children tend to pick up stuff fast, and they can start with the very basic tasks. Some ideas for getting them to pitch in:

• Give very small children a **toy knife and some offcuts from ingredients**; they can imitate you while you work.

• **Washing vegetables**: what child doesn't love water?

• **Mixing ingredients in a bowl:** of course it might need a quick stir from you to finish off, and it might not all stay in the bowl but practice makes perfect!

• **Lining baking tins:** scissor work is excellent for fine motor skills.

• **Kneading and rolling:** dough is especially forgiving of small hands.

• **Older children can start to peel, grate and chop**, but keep a careful eye on anything sharp.

• **Weighing out ingredients:** great for maths (and they won't even know it!).

• **Reading the recipe aloud to you at each step:** again, helping with words without even noticing!

AND AFTERWARDS...
CLEARING UP TOGETHER

That moment when everyone leaves the table and the magic fairies fail to appear? It's when many hands make light work and the job can be done in no time at all, giving everyone a longer evening break afterwards. Leaving one person to do it all breeds resentment, not to mention exhaustion, so keep the kitchen your positive space by making it a team effort. Assign jobs according to age, and if there are complaints about who does what, agree a rota. At the very least, it's a good habit to get children into clearing plates and dishes off the table and stacking them in the dishwasher. There are usually other jobs apart from washing and clearing up, such as decanting leftovers into tubs for the fridge, and not forgetting the finishing touch of wiping the table – a clean and clear space to greet you the following morning.

Can we just all eat the same?

In an ideal world, everyone would tuck into the same dishes. But the reality is that sometimes one person is vegan, one hates fish and someone else is gluten intolerant. How can you possibly cater for everyone at once? The extra work in cooking separate meals, plus the added expense (and the washing up...) are draining even before you even start. While you can't always produce a one-pot dish to suit everyone, there are ways to avoid having to prepare an array of completely separate dishes for every meal. Keeping it as simple as possible, cooking from scratch, will save you time, money and sanity.

• Start with the positives: make a list of all the dishes you CAN all eat.

• Then write a list of the dishes that have one or two ingredients that make them unsuitable for everyone: these can be substituted, or tweaked – you'll find plenty of ideas for this in the recipes in this book.

• Have optional extras on the table, so everyone can customise their own plate. Offer extra chilli for the spice fiend. Have meat or cheese on the side rather than part of the main dish.

• With fussy eaters, pack in the stuff you know they do like and it will distract from the odd bit of veg they claim they don't like.

• Picking out and rejecting bits isn't to be encouraged, but neither is it the end of the world – it's usually a phase that runs its course if ignored.

Vegetarian & vegan diets

Following a vegetarian diet for most means not eating meat, poultry and fish, while dairy and eggs are ok. Some also avoid foods made using animal-based by-products, such as rennet (used in some cheeses) and gelatine. Vegans avoid any products deriving from animals, which includes all dairy and eggs as well as meat and fish, and also honey.

Turning vegetarian or vegan is a switch that more and more people are making, for reasons that include environmental, animal welfare and health. It is estimated that around 14% of adults (7.2 million) in the UK follow a meat-free diet, and around 7% of the UK population (around 3.5 million people) follow a vegan one, with the numbers rising over the last couple of years and continuing in that direction. And unless the whole family goes down the same route, you won't always be eating the same as each other. But that's not to say you can't keep everyone happy most of the time, without a load of extra stress.

Living life on the veg

It can be easy to cater for vegetarians within a meat-eating family. Since most of us could do with cutting down on our meat consumption, for health as well as environmental reasons, establishing one or two meat-free days each week is a good place to start. You could even plan for a special vegetarian (or vegan) week from time to time. Meat, poultry and fish are all relatively expensive and can add quite a bit to your food shop, so sticking to grains, pulses and veg will do your wallet a favour too. You'll also find that 5-a-day easy to hit on a non-meat day.

Food allergies & intolerances

When cooking in a household that includes someone with a food allergy, who is at risk of a serious reaction from certain foods, then it is vital to avoid the trigger food. Cooking from scratch is the best way to have peace of mind as to what is going into each dish – no more agonised scrutiny of ingredient lists. You have complete control over what you are putting into your dishes and mouths, and knowing they are completely safe for everyone.

A food intolerance, as distinct from an allergy, relates to difficulty digesting certain foods, and having an unpleasant physical reaction to them. These can include tummy pain and bloating as well as skin rashes and itching. Food intolerances are not always easy to identify, and it's always best to see your GP if you have persistent symptoms.

While it can be trickier to find dishes for the whole family when one person has an allergy or intolerance, that's when meal planning (see page 15) really comes into its own. Get everyone involved in finding dishes that suit everyone, or that can be tweaked here and there to exclude any of the offending ingredients.

IS A VEGAN DIET SAFE FOR CHILDREN?

Yes, as long as parents are well informed on how to ensure no key nutrients are lacking (especially protein, vitamins B12 and D, calcium, iron and omega-3 fatty acids). Research in 2021 found that 8% of children in the UK aged 5–16 were following a vegan diet and a further 15% said they would like to. For more information, visit www.bbcgoodfood.com/howto/guide/vegan-diet-healthy-kids.

Sources
https://www.vegansociety.com/news/media/statistics/families-and-children
https://www.finder.com/uk/uk-diet-trends

FOR VEGETARIAN-FRIENDLY MEALS

1. To keep the meat-eaters happy too, **pick something you can make meat-free, with optional add-ons**: customised pizzas, for instance (see page 132), or Teriyaki Beef Stir Fry (see page 140) – keep the beef separate until you serve, and maybe add in a little tofu as protein for the veggie/vegan option.

2. **Recreate family favourites using meat substitutes:** use quick and easy canned pulses to make your favourite chilli (see page 110) or soya mince in place of beef mince in a classic lasagne or spaghetti bolognaise.

3. **Instead of spending on a takeaway curry, save yourself the money and make a night in of it.** Cook up a few simple dishes – either all vegetarian, or include one meat dish in the mix. Everyone is sharing the same meal, but sticking to their own dietary choice and needs.

Catering for vegans

- A vegan diet can be less calorie-dense, so vegans need to eat more in quantity to get enough energy.
- Watch out for quality as well as quantity, and that all the necessary nutrients are covered. Visit https://www.nhs.uk/live-well/eat-well/the-vegan-diet for tips on healthy vegan eating.
- It takes a little more planning, but these days there are plenty of meat and dairy substitutes around that make most traditional dishes easy to recreate.
- Try out a few brands of substitute ingredients – they can be very different – and you'll soon find your favourites.

Cut
the waste

It is estimated that UK households throw away over 6 million tonnes of food each year, an amount that would fill about 66,000 three-bedroom terraced houses. 4.5 million tonnes of that is classified as food that could have been eaten, worth about £14 billion and equating to around £60 per month for the average family. That's eight meals a week, straight into the bin. And while things are certainly moving in the right direction, there are adjustments we can all make to minimise food waste in our own homes – for the sake the environment as much as our wallets.

It starts at home

We may not feel we have much control over the bigger picture, but we all have a small part to play, and plenty of good reasons to keep a lid on food waste. If you spend money on something you don't use and then throw away, that's throwing money away. It's that simple. Eliminating food waste completely is a challenge, but cutting it right down is something we can all get behind.

Smart shopping

Think ahead and buy only what you need. Which means planning your meals, making a list, checking your cupboards and fridge before you go shopping, then sticking to the list. It's not the end of the world if you find you are missing something later in the week – top-up shops are all but inevitable, and better than buying more in case and then having to throw it away. See page 15 for our tips on how to shop for just the food you need and not the food you don't.

When it's gone, it's gone

There will always be items that creep past their use-by date without you noticing, and when binning them is the only option. **For fresh goods**, the use-by date is a matter of food safety (see page 12) and if it's gone past the date, it's not safe to eat. Remember too that not all fridges are kept at the same temperature or level of efficiency, so if your cream cheese date says it's good to go but it looks iffy, don't risk it. Always err on the side of caution, especially where meat or dairy are concerned.

'If you spend money on something you don't use and then throw away, that's throwing money away.'

- **For things marked best-before**, though, you need to use a little judgement... in other words your eyes and nose. **Golden rule: if it smells bad, it is bad.** Mould (except on blue cheese) is a no-no, so if there is any on your bread, bin it. Just turning stale, though, and it's fine to use. If **eggs** have passed their best-before date, place in a bowl of water – if they sink they are good; if they float they are bad. **For veg on the turn**, take a close look – you might be able to trim off any ends turning bad, and what's left will be fine to use.

- **Dry goods**, such as flour, sugar, chocolate and pulses, and general store cupboard items, will last for anything from a few months to a year. How you store them will determine how long they last – a cool, dark place as ideal. Heat and humidity will shorten their lifespan, so avoid keeping them in cupboards next to the cooker or boiler. Make sure packets are sealed or properly resealed, and go through them from time to time to see if anything could do with using up soon. Again, it's a matter of judgement rather than safety here, and a quick sniff, taste or feel will usually give you a good enough idea. **Dried spices and herbs** won't go off, but they definitely lose their zing, so buy them in small quantities.

Source
https://wrap.org.uk/resources/report/food-surplus-and-waste-uk-key-facts

STORE IT RIGHT

As soon as you get the shopping home, storing it all properly,
and without delay, means it will keep for longer.

IN THE FRIDGE

• Put all **raw meat**, **poultry** and **fish** on the bottom shelf to avoid contaminating other foods.
• **Eggs:** you can keep these at room temperature but they will last longer if refrigerated.
• **Fruit and veg**, with the exception of: potatoes, onions, garlic and citrus.
• Remove **fresh herbs** from their packets, trim off their stems and store in water, changing the water every few days. Keep the water level low, and take care not to spill any in the fridge.
• If you are buying **new items**, such as yoghurt, before old ones are finished, make sure you bring the opened ones to the front so you use them up first.

IN THE FREEZER

• Apart from the obvious frozen items, also consider any **multi-buy deals on fresh food** that you bought into – will you be using that food or are they better off in the freezer for a later date?
• **Storing food by type** (veg, bread, ice cream, portions of batch-cooked food etc.) makes it a lot easier to find things in the freezer and to check what you have at a glance.
• It's worth doing the odd **stock-take and clear-out of your freezer**, to see what needs eating soon. To avoid reaching the binning stage, though, bring older items to the tops of the drawers as you add new ones.

FOR FREEZING EGGS

You might often find you have leftover yolks or whites, or even unused whole eggs, and they will all freeze for up to a year. Don't forget to label, and always fully defrost eggs (ideally in the fridge) before cooking with them.

1. Don't freeze whole eggs in their shells – they will crack! Beat together to combine, then freeze in a suitable container (allowing room for expansion).

2. Freeze whites as they are, or gently mixed together.

3. Yolks need to be frozen with an extra ingredient to prevent them turning sticky when defrosted. Mix with either a little sugar or salt – for 4 yolks, 1½ tsp sugar or a pinch of salt – according to how you intend to use them later.

USE OR LOSE?

- **Store any leftovers in sealed containers** in the fridge, ready to reheat (see page 20).
- **If you only use half a can of food**, decant the remainder into a container, cover and keep chilled.
- **Wrapping opened food properly** prolongs its life and stops it drying out – cheese, for example, is best double wrapped in baking parchment.
- **If you don't use a whole piece of vegetable or fruit**, don't automatically throw out the rest. Half a carrot might look a little lost, but there's a sauce or stew waiting to welcome it. Or just munch it.**Rescue remedy**: veg lurking in the fridge and starting to look less than perky can be turned into wholesome soup.
- **Odds and ends**: don't write off the less obvious veg parts – broccoli and cauliflower stems are as edible as the florets, and good in soups.
- **Do you need to peel it?** Often much of the goodness is in the skin – better in your body than in the bin. Potatoes and carrots can be scrubbed instead of peeled, and all but the toughest-skinned winter squashes have peel that is delicious left on and roasted.
- **Consider a 'leftovers dinner' occasionally**: rootle through the fridge and freezer and get out anything that looks in need of some love. It might be a bit of an odd, mismatched dinner, but it's chance to get creative. And if it turns out weird... well, it's a one-off!
- If you have **too much milk approaching its use-by date**, freeze it and defrost it for the day you know you will use it. Remember that liquids expand as they freeze, so don't freeze a full container.

USING UP ODDS & ENDS

- **Parmesan rinds:** wrap and keep in the fridge, then drop them into broths, soups or tomato sauces as they cook (fish them out at the end) – they add depth of flavour.
- **Stale bread:** blitz into breadcrumbs and freeze for later use. Or simply toast it.
- **Leftover cooked veg:** upcycle by adding to soups, frittatas (see page 98) or salads.
- **Chicken carcasses and bones:** boil up bones with a few veg and aromatics (onion, carrot, bay leaf, peppercorns) and simmer for a couple of hours to make stock. Strain then freeze in ice-cube trays, ready to add to soups and stews.

And you do have to throw it away...

Council food waste schemes: many local authorities offer weekly food waste collections, along with the usual recycling. You can throw pretty much anything into the caddy provided, including raw and cooked meat, veg peelings, scrapings from everyone's plates, anything turning mouldy... the lot. It can get turned into green energy for powering homes, and green fertilisers for farmland. Plans are moving for every household in the country to have access to the scheme, so look out for your caddy and make a point of using it.

Making your own compost: if you have any outdoor space for growing plants, even just a window box, then making your own compost saves money and cuts down on waste. There are plenty of websites out there that can show you how to turn your veg peelings and scraps into nutrient-rich compost that your plants will love.

Store cupboard staples

A well-stocked store cupboard means you will always be able to rustle something up with short notice – no need to dash to the shops or scroll down the takeaway menu. With just a core set of staples, you can knock out a range of inexpensive and delicious dishes in no time at all. Many people are now choosing a plant-based diet, so have a good selection of ingredients to accommodate those needs and you have all bases covered.

Pasta, rice, noodles & grains

Have a few different pasta shapes to hand, and if you finish one and start another in the same pan, check they have the same cooking time. **Basmati or long grain** – wholegrain or white – will fit the bill in most instances, both as an accompaniment and in a range of recipes, including kedgeree (see page 46). Risotto rice comes in handy too, and is what gives the dish its special creamy consistency.

Dried noodles in your cupboard mean you are never far from a tasty bowl of goodness. Rice (ribbon or vermicelli) udon or egg noodles are great for Asian dishes and stir fries, and soba (buckwheat) bring a wholesome, nutty character to a dish.

Couscous, including the wholewheat variety, is another versatile ingredient that is ready in a matter of minutes. Other handy, wholesome grains include **pearl barley** and **quinoa**.

Oils & vinegars

Keep a store of **vegetable, groundnut or rapeseed oil** for cooking and frying, and **olive oil** for coating, cooking and drizzling. Have a nice **extra-virgin olive oil** to save for dressings and a final drizzle over a dish. **Balsamic, cider and wine vinegar** are all great in dressings, marinades and sauces, and each brings its own character.

Herbs & spices

You don't need every single dried spice and herb in your store cupboard and since they don't last indefinitely, stick to the ones that you are likely to use most – think about **curry powder, cumin, coriander, cardamom pods, turmeric, ginger, smoked paprika, dried chilli flakes, five-spice, cinnamon and mixed spice, plus fennel seeds, dried oregano, dried thyme** and **bay leaves.** Buy in small quantities and refresh regularly, expanding your range as you go. There are some great spice mixes out there that add instant flavour to marinades, and that save you having to buy and store all the individual spices in the mix.

Tins & jars

Tinned pulses, tomatoes, fish, coconut milk and **fruit** all have an important place in your store cupboard – see page 36 for more on which are the most useful.

If you don't have time to start it from scratch, a jar of your favourite **curry paste** means you can rustle up a curry in next to no time. **Roasted red peppers** can find many uses (see the Smoked Fish Burgers on page 180), and a jar of your favourite pesto is a welcome find on a rushed weekday evening. **Jalapeños** add a chilli flourish to salsas, and as a garnish.

Baking ingredients

Have **self-raising** and **plain flour,** plus **cornflour, baking powder** and **bicarbonate of soda** on hand for baking, batters and thickening. **Wholemeal flour** has a shorter shelf life, but is a healthier option and adds flavour and texture (see the crêpes on page 55). Although many doughs, especially flatbread, are made with plain or self-raising, if you are making a traditional loaf, then **bread flour** will give best results. If you also have a small stash of **dried yeast** in the cupboard, you are ready to get kneading.

Cocoa powder (unsweetened) and **vanilla extract** bring rich flavours to many sweet foods, and although vanilla is expensive, a little goes a long way.

Caster, granulated and **icing sugar** are your store cupboard staples for general use in baking and desserts, while **soft light brown sugar** adds a lovely caramel flavour.

You'll find **porridge oats** in many of the recipes in this book – breakfast bowls, granola, smoothies, cookies and sweet traybakes, even savoury muffins. Highly nutritious and adaptable, giving slow-release energy, they also happen to be inexpensive. Rolled, smooth, jumbo and plain oats all have their different uses, but you can often swap them in for each other.

Nuts & seeds

Keep some of your favourites in jars for toasting and sprinkling over everything from salads and soups to breakfast porridge and yoghurt. Also for blitzing into a pesto or adding nutritious crunch to baked treats. **Flaked almonds** are very versatile, adding texture and flavour to both savoury and sweet dishes.

Seasonings, flavourings & condiments

Sea salt is a natural product and not expensive – keep fine for cooking and flakes for sprinkling. Have **black peppercorns** for grinding fresh as needed, as ready ground loses its flavour quite quickly. **Soy sauce** adds a delicious savoury depth to marinades, sauces and finished dishes. Seek out low-salt options, which still give you that flavour hit, and check the label as many contain wheat, making them unsuitable for a gluten-free diet.

Chicken and vegetable **stock cubes** are super-handy for bringing instant flavour to soups and stews – opting for the low-salt versions means you are then in control of salt levels in the finished dish. **Tomato purée** adds concentrated flavour to sauces and stews without introducing more liquid. **Onion granules** are an instant way to distribute onion flavour throughout a dish or bake. **Worcestershire sauce** adds a boost to stews, sauces and marinades – it traditionally contains anchovies, but vegetarian and vegan versions are available, so check the label if need be.

Keep a selection of your favourite condiments, such as **mayonnaise, ketchup, brown sauce, chilli sauce** and **mustard**, but remember that most need to be stored in the fridge once opened.

VEGAN & VEGETARIAN STORE CUPBOARD

Vegans in particular need to make sure they are including in their diet all the nutrients needed to stay healthy. As the number of people choosing a plant-based diet has increased dramatically over recent years, so the range, and easy availability, of food suitable for vegetarians and vegans has exploded – including in the ready-meal aisle. But just because it's plant-based doesn't automatically mean it's healthy, and cooking from scratch is still the best, and cheapest, way to ensure you know exactly what you are eating and getting. Happily, there is no shortage of vegan-friendly ingredients and products out there for creating your own delicious dishes that don't have to compromise on flavour.

Wholewheat pasta & noodles, & brown rice

Eating more whole grains is good for all of our health. Including them regularly in your diet may reduce your risk of heart disease, type 2 diabetes and obesity, especially when they are replacing refined grains. While filling you up for longer, they can also improve your digestive health. You may find that you come to prefer their flavour, too. Be aware, though, that anyone with a gluten intolerance should avoid wheat, barley and rye.

For people on plant-based diets they are a key staple, as many of the nutrients found in whole grains are less available in other plant-based foods – especially iron, B vitamins and zinc. Opting for **wholewheat pasta** and **noodles**, and **brown rice**, instead of the refined white versions, is a simple way to boost your nutrient intake.

NUT BUTTERS

Remember when it was just peanut butter? Well, now **almond, cashew,** even **hazelnut, soy nut** and **sunflower seed** have been added to the shelves, and the great news is that they are all good for you, containing nutrients that are particularly important if you follow a plant-based diet. Nuts are an excellent source of protein, fibre and healthy fats, and also contain a range of minerals and vitamins, including vitamin E, which supports your immune system as well as healthy skin and hair. Read the label, though, as not all nut butters are created equal. You might want to avoid any that have added salt, sugar and palm oil and stick instead to the ones that are pure nuts.

PLANT-BASED MILKS

The last few years have seen the availability and variety of plant-based milks skyrocket. Most have similar calcium and vitamin D levels to cows' milk, and many have added vitamins and minerals for an extra boost. Some people find they prefer one type over another for tea or coffee, then a different one for cooking. It's a question of trying out a few to see what works for you – you'll find **almond, soya, oat, coconut, rice, hazelnut** and **cashew**, even **pea** and **hemp.** Check the ingredients, though, as not all are unsweetened. Unopened, most plant-based milks can be stored for up to a year at room temperature, so keeping a steady supply in the store cupboard means you don't have to worry about running out or wastage. Once opened they need to be stored in the fridge, where they have a shelf life similar to dairy milk, if not a little longer.

Natural sweeteners

You'll notice from our recipes in this book that we don't reach for the refined sugar in order to rustle up something sweet, opting instead for more natural versions. Although these are less refined, they do still have the same calorie content, and will have the same effect on your teeth as regular sugar. But as well containing small traces of antioxidants and minerals, we find they just taste much better; you won't need to use as much of them to hit that sweet flavour spot.

Maple syrup brings more than just a delicious sweetness – it's also a good source of antioxidants and essential minerals, including calcium and zinc. **Date syrup** is another caramelly, natural sweetener and is rich in minerals and vitamins. Both can be used in place of honey, or as a healthier alternative to sugar when sweetening dishes. **Agave syrup**, or nectar, is another natural alternative, and has some health benefits over sugar, but is more processed and refined than date or maple syrup. While most vegans do not eat **honey**, vegetarians can enjoy it as a natural sweetener – look for 'raw' on the label, as this means it will come from a single source, has had nothing added and will not have been heat treated (heat destroys its beneficial enzymes).

Flavour enhancers

For plant-based diets especially, an extra kick is sometimes called for in order to add the depth of flavour that meat and dairy can bring to a dish. Luckily, there are various flavour enhancers out there that are instant providers of this savoury boost, or 'umami' (the fifth taste after sweet, salty, sour and bitter).

Nutritional yeast – essentially dried flakes of yeast where the yeast has been de-activated – is a highly nutritious vegan product and a good source of protein and B vitamins. It has a nutty, cheesy flavour, making it ideal to sprinkle over pasta dishes, or to add a 'meaty' kick to vegetarian and vegan dishes. **Liquid aminos** are concentrated amino acids (proteins) made from soybeans and water. Vegan and gluten free, they can be used as an alternative to soy sauce, or added in small amounts to dishes to boost salty, savoury flavours. **Yeast extract** (aka Marmite) might divide the population when it comes to spreading it on toast, but a spoonful here and there in stews, sauces and even breads, will add an umami hit similar to liquid aminos. **Miso paste** – a traditional Japanese seasoning made from fermented soy beans – is a good source of antioxidants, fibre and protein, and also adds umami to broths and Asian-style dishes.

DARK CHOCOLATE

It's official: it's good for us! Dark chocolate (with at least 70% cocoa solids) is generally vegan, but check the label as they are not all necessarily dairy free. Useful in baking and desserts, but also for nibbling...

tips

FOR STORE CUPBOARD

1.
Keep an eye on stocks, and make sure anything running low goes on the next shopping list.

2.
For long-life items, and especially tins, buy however much you have space for so you don't need to add them to every shop.

3.
Take the occasional look at your best-before dates – flours, for example (and especially wholemeal) do go off.

4.
Check the labels for storage advice: many things can be stored in the cupboard indefinitely, but once opened need to go in the fridge.

5.
Buy spices and dried herbs in small amounts and replenish regularly so they don't lose their zing.

6.
Try to stick to the same brands for things like pasta, noodles and rice, so you can mix old and new packets and cook at the same time.

7.
When unloading a shop, place newer items at the back of the cupboard and bring older ones to the front, so you use them first.

8.
Seal any opened packets with a sturdy clip, or decant into airtight jars.

9.
If decanting into storage containers, **don't add new food to the existing stock** – wait until you use up the last of what you have.

YES
WE CAN

A cupboard stacked with tinned food will come to your rescue time and again. Instant goodness, cooked and ready to go, generally cheap, plus a long shelf life and easy to store – what's not to like? There are cookbooks (and even a festival!) devoted entirely to cooking with tins, and it's easy to see why – their versatility means you can whip up a salad, soup or stew in next to no time. While baked beans and tinned tomatoes are the top two best-sellers in the UK, and fantastic in their own right (see below), there's a world of delectable possibility beyond them.

Take your pulse

First up, magic beans. Dried pulses are all well and good, and can work out cheaper, but they mostly need overnight soaking and a long, slow simmer. Compare that to opening a tin and tipping the contents into a sieve for a quick drain and rinse: a pile of perfectly cooked goodness ready to go. High in fibre and protein and low in fat, pulses aren't just great for plant-based diets. They can transform from something quite ordinary into a mouth-watering and healthy dish. Cooked tinned pulses are also great for bulking out a meat stew or chilli, as well as for adding substance to soups and salads, and they play a starring role in many of the recipes in this book.

So what pulses are we talking about? **Chickpeas, lentils (brown and green), cannellini, haricot, adzuki, kidney, black eye, borlotti, pinto, butter beans, black beans...** it's one big, happy family! Check the label and buy only those canned in water rather than brine (which is salty), or any flavoured sauce (which might play havoc with the flavours in a recipe).

When talking pulses, there's no forgetting the great national favourite: **baked beans**. And while you might not think of them as a 'health food', like all pulses they are high in fibre

and protein and a good source of B vitamins and low in fat, and are one of your 5-a-day. Reduced-salt and -sugar versions are available and, in terms of price, it's worth trying out a few brands.

THREE CHEERS FOR CHICKPEAS

Of all the pulses, perhaps the most adaptable and universally loved is the chickpea. And no more so than when it appears in houmous form. It's hard to find anyone who doesn't like houmous – its creamy, garlicky and nutty flavour appeals to all ages, from early weaning stages upwards. Look out for variations – you'll find everything from Moroccan spiced or lemony to beetroot or pea – or blitz up some of your own. Perfect as a dip, or inside a pitta or sandwich, houmous has even found its way into pasta sauces and pizza toppings.

Chickpeas don't stop at houmous, though – try them spiced and grilled or roasted, such as for the sweet jacket potato filling on page 85, thrown into salads, in a curry or combined with lentils in a dahl (see page 138), or added to a stew or gumbo (see page 149).

Your go-to tinned pulse dishes
Soups – Tomato and Bean Soup (see page 86)
Chilli – Veggie BBQ Chilli (see page 108)
Salsa – Jamaican-style Taco salsa (see page 166)
Houmous – it doesn't have to be chickpeas...
   try the Butter Bean Houmous (see page 76)
Dahl – Quick-cook Dahl (see page 138)
Veggie pies – Mushroom and Lentil Pie
   (see page 109)

Plenty of other fish

Tuna is an incredibly versatile store cupboard stand-by, turning up in salads, sandwiches, pasta bakes, jacket potatoes and tuna melts, to name but a few. It's also high in protein and omega-3 fatty acids (good for heart health). It is canned in either brine, spring water or oil – brine is salty and oil adds extra fat, so opt for spring water. **Salmon**, which shares tuna's health profile, is less expensive canned than fresh but has all the same health benefits and versatility – in fishcakes, pasta dishes, salads or tarts. **Anchovies** are concentrated flavour bombs that enrich sauces and dressings.

Fruit

While eating fresh fruit is always preferable, tinned fruit can still be part of your 5-a-day, and as long as it's canned in its own juice rather than sugary syrup, is a healthy option. Keep a selection – **pineapple, cherries, peaches** or **pears** – and you will always have a quick dessert or fruity addition to a breakfast bowl of yoghurt, cereal or porridge, or try the Power Punch (see page 45).

DOWN THE DRAIN

Most recipes call for pulses to be drained and rinsed, but there are times you might want to think before you tip. The liquid from a can of chickpeas is called aquafaba and, as vegans across the world have discovered, can be a handy substitute for egg whites, since it whips into a thick cream. Black beans come in a rich, dark liquid that can often be added to a dish as it cooks, so drain them into a jug rather than down the sink and that way you have the liquid reserved should you need it.

OPENED CANS

If you only use some of a tin of food, never leave the remainder in the can for storage, as once the food is open to the air, the tin from the can might transfer to the contents, introducing toxins. Decant any leftovers into a small container, cover and store for a few days in the fridge.

Tomatoes & vegetables

Where would we be without the humble **tinned tomato**? Cheap, available everywhere, but amazingly versatile and a key ingredient in so many dishes. Chopped tomatoes are a time saver, but if you prefer whole and want the option of using the tomatoes and juice separately, simply snip them up roughly using kitchen scissors when a recipe calls for chopped. Quality can vary, and it's not necessarily linked to price, so shop around until you find your favourite brand – generally speaking, the richer the juices the further your tins will stretch.

Eating plenty of fresh veg is really important, but that's not to say the odd can in your cupboard won't come in handy now and again, and can save you precious time. See page 65 for a spicy egg recipe that uses a tin of potatoes to bulk out the other veg. **Sweetcorn** is another store cupboard winner – generally popular with children, it's a good way to add appeal, as well as colour, to a dish they might otherwise baulk at (see the veggie chilli on page 108).

Coconut milk

Coconut milk turns a curry or soup beautifully creamy and tempers any fierce chilli heat. But don't save it for Asian-style dishes and curries – its creamy quality makes it ideal in desserts, as many vegans are aware... Go for light versions, as you will still get all the nutrients and flavour but with less fat.

Breakfast
& lunch
on the go

We know that skipping breakfast before a day of school or work is not the best start to the day, but the frantic morning dash means that breakfast is often a meal eaten on the hoof rather than at the table. With a bit of thinking ahead, organisation and a few sturdy containers, you can look forward to nutritious and money-saving breakfasts and lunches every day.

Kickstarting the day

Maybe you are someone who doesn't feel like eating as soon as you wake up? Making breakfast a portable meal means you get to eat when you want, and once your tastebuds (and you!) are fully awake. Sitting around the table together first thing isn't always an option for busy families with different schedules; leisurely breakfasts and brunches are for the weekend. But on-the-go doesn't have to mean grabbing the nearest snack. Tempting cereal bars can be marketed as a wholesome breakfast alternative, but they sometimes contain saturated fat and added sugar. And the cost can mount up.

There are plenty of fresh ideas for a nutritious start to your day that won't add to the morning stress, and will do your wallet a favour at the same time. Some of these are just a question of getting a bit organised the night before, or making sure you have plenty of fruit in the freezer and fruit bowl. And a spot of weekend baking and freezing in advance can be your morning friend.

PACKED & READY

Invest in a good selection of lidded containers for transporting your lunch, and keep them somewhere handy. That way you won't be rummaging in cupboards or resorting to old yoghurt pots. A range of sizes means you can pack everything neatly in the right sized tub, keeping everything compact, as well as easier to carry with you. Choose ones that are dishwasher and microwave safe, and that have a good seal, especially if you plan to transport liquids.

ON-THE-GO BREAKFAST IDEAS

- **Ditch the commercial cereal bars** and make your own – that way you choose exactly what goes into them (see the recipes in this book). Make them in weekly batches to cut down on the work – or batch bake and store in the freezer.
- **Think outside the (cereal) box and branch out.** Savoury or sweet muffins (see page 58) are a great way to start the day, as well as being super portable.
- **Go liquid.** Get a head start on your 5-a-day and opt for a home-made smoothie or fruity punch (see pages 67 and 45).
- **Pack up a Porridge Pot the night before** (see page 60) then all you have to do is add boiling water, plus any fresh extras, whenever you are ready. Or **soak your oats overnight** (see page 66), grab a handful of fruit and tuck in once you get to your workplace.

School lunchboxes

There's a world of pre-packaged snacks aimed at children and their time-poor parents, and maybe it's not necessarily the healthiest choice. Making sure children eat well in the middle of their learning day matters to all of us, but how do you find food that will do them good and that they are happy to eat? Relying on packaged snacks eases the strain, but it often isn't a healthy option. Nor a cheap one – the cost of individually wrapped items can really stack up over the week, or term. And all that single-use plastic comes at a price too – to all of us, down the line. But we have some handy tips...

Be realistic

If lunch comes home untouched, it doesn't matter how good or healthy it is if it's heading for the bin. Finding healthy foods your child will eat might mean a little bit of negotiation and compromise.

Slowly does it

Children can be resistant to change, so switching out everything at once in their lunchbox might be too much. Introduce the changes gradually – a crisp swap here, a fruit addition there – and you are more likely to get them onside.

Set an example

Children are learning and setting lifelong habits in their daily routines, and making lunch not just healthy but something to look forward to will benefit them later in life. Pack yourself the same lunch occasionally, even if you will be eating it separately. You could even pack the lunchboxes up together.

Keep it simple

With your main family meal in the evening, keep the focus on that and don't feel you have to produce anything fancy for lunch. Packing in hundreds of mini items really isn't necessary – a couple of sandwiches or a wrap, plus a piece of fruit and possibly a sweet treat (ideally home-made) will get most children through the day. And will take minutes to put together.

SCHOOL LUNCHBOX IDEAS

- Sandwiches don't always tick the box, so switch it up and **fill a pitta or wrap** instead – customise the fillings by getting everyone to suggest or, better still, do their own.
- **Explore new fillings:** it's easy to get stuck in a ham rut, but a little variety goes a long way and can mean healthier options: try houmous, cream cheese or pesto as a starting point, adding grated carrot, pepper strips and salad.
- **Look beyond the bread:** ring the changes with frittata, noodles or pasta.
- **Make extra of any favourite dinner** and pop it into a lunchbox for the following day. Noodles, pizza and pasta usually hit the spot with children, even cold.
- **Beware mini packs** of savoury snacks, which can be laden with salt and high in saturated fat – they can fill you up at the cost of healthier options. They aren't all bad, though, so check the packet, and consider making them a once-a-week treat.
- **Lunch is great for getting in some of your 5-a-day.** Apples, plums, bananas, carrot sticks, grapes and cherry tomatoes (cut into pieces for younger children, to avoid choking) will all survive the journey to school.
- A healthy lunch doesn't mean completely sugar free. **Include a treat but make it home-made.** You'll find great recipes in this book for home bakes that can be sliced and transported, and you can even bake them together.

Sweet lunchbox treat ideas
Store-cupboard Cookies (see page 192)
Peanut Butter and Date Flapjacks
    (see page 190) – but check nut regulations
    at your school
Oat, Date and Nut Power Bars (see page 50)
Blueberry, Oat and Orange Snack Bars
    (see page 51)
Sweet Muffins (see page 58)
Chocolate and Raspberry Twists (see page 158)

Work lunch on the go

In the middle of the working day, lunch is the time to relish a quiet moment and some well-earned, effort-free food. Nipping out to your favourite outlet can become a comforting daily routine, but buying lunch every day comes at a cost, adding up to a huge annual spend. Much like takeaway dinners, seeing it as an occasional treat rather than day-to-day solution puts you more in control of your budget as well as what you eat.

Get ahead

Making lunch from scratch before leaving the house in the morning is for the super-organised. For everyone else, a little planning the night before means all you have to do the next day is open the fridge, grab a container or two, and a fork, and you're good to go.

• **Make friends with your leftovers.** Rather than rely on there being any, plan for them and make extra the night before. Decant some of your dish before you sit down for dinner, to make sure it isn't accidentally snaffled as second helpings...

• When planning your weekly meals, **think about lunches the following day** – Friday is not the ideal night for eating something that works well in a lunchbox.

• **Make leftovers stretch further** by stuffing them into a wrap or pitta. Roasted veg, houmous, leftover chicken or veggie chilli... there isn't much that doesn't taste even better upcycled into a wrap.

• If putting together ingredients from scratch, **do as much as you can the night before** – for example, if taking noodles, you could cook them in advance then just add your preferred flavourings in the morning.

• **Have enough suitable, sealable containers,** in handy sizes, to transport your lunch in.

Club together

If you have friendly colleagues, why not pool resources and share the load? You could take it in turns to bring in double portions some days. It's a great way to try new ideas for your own lunches. And it turns the lunch break into a sociable affair, while giving you a day off lunch prep.

WORK
LUNCHBOX
IDEAS

• **Salads**: from a simple combo of lettuce, cucumber and tomato to a more hearty grain-laden assembly, most are highly portable. Take any dressing separately and hold it back until just before you eat, to avoid soggy leaves. The Greek Couscous Salad (see page 78), Tuna Niçoise (see page 82), or Chicken, Spelt and Pepper Salad (see page 101) are all good starting points.

• **Soup it up**. An inexpensive vacuum flask means you can take hot soup to work (or transport cold if you can reheat it at the office) – a filling, highly nutritious and cheap lunch. See Tomato and Bean (see page 86) or, for a cold winter's day, Leek and Potato (see page 94).

• Great eaten cold, **noodles** are highly portable and a perfect vehicle for Asian-style flavours. Add raw or cooked veg and/or cooked meat or fish to rice noodles, and take a soy-based dressing in a separate pot. See page 72 for a delicious Poke Bowl.

• Most **pasta dishes** are either good served up cold, or given a quick warm through. Try the Chickpea and Basil Pesto Pasta on page 112 for a nutrient-packed lunch that will see you through the afternoon.

• **Fresh fruit**, **nuts** and **dried fruit** are brilliant sweet hits for when energy levels are flagging throughout the day, but if the temptation is to reach for a chocolate bar, have a home-made bar at the ready. It will keep you perkier for longer than a quick sugar spike.

brunch
time

menu

Holly's Power Punch *45*

Smoked Haddock Kedgeree *46*

Ultimate Omelette *49*

Oat, Date and Nut Power Bars *50*

Blueberry, Oat and Orange Snack Bars *51*

Fruity Crêpes *55*

Baked Spiced Honey and Apple Porridge *56*

Two-way Muffins *58*

Apple and Cinnamon Porridge Pots *60*

Oaty Smoothie *61*

Coconut and Orange Granola *62*

One-pan Spicy Eggs *65*

Banana Chocolate Overnight Oats *66*

Super Green Smoothie *67*

Green tea is a great way to start the day. Blitzing it with some tinned fruit means you've already ticked off one of your 5-a-day before breakfast. This makes enough for 3 days, so just store it in the fridge in drinks bottles and you have one ready to grab and go.

Holly's Power Punch

2 green tea bags
400ml boiling water
160g drained tinned pears
    in fruit juice
80g drained tinned peaches
    in fruit juice

Place the tea bags in a heatproof jug, pour over the boiling water and leave to steep for 2 minutes.

Meanwhile, tip the tinned pears and peaches into a blender and blitz to as fine a purée as possible.

Strain in the steeped tea and blitz once more, then decant into 3 sealable containers and chill until needed. It will keep in the fridge for up to 3 days.

This works well with many different fruit combinations. Try peaches and black cherries, apple and blackberry, or even pineapple and mango. Just pick your two favourite tinned fruits and get blending – remember to choose the fruits that are tinned in natural juice.

This kedgeree takes very little time to bring together, but packs a flavour punch with the cinnamon, bay leaves and curry powder. The fish steams on top of the rice and you can choose to serve it as a portion each, or you can flake it through the rice.

Smoked Haddock Kedgeree

1 tsp vegetable oil
2 red onions, finely chopped
1 red pepper, deseeded and
    roughly chopped
2 tbsp medium curry powder
1 tsp ground cinnamon
2 bay leaves
750ml boiling water
1 reduced-salt vegetable
    stock cube
375g basmati rice, rinsed
3 eggs
200g frozen peas
finely grated zest and juice
    of 1 lemon
2 tbsp roughly chopped
    flat-leaf parsley
400g skinless and boneless
    undyed smoked haddock
freshly ground black pepper,
    to taste

Heat a large sauté pan or saucepan until medium hot. Add the oil and onions and cook, stirring, over a low heat for 5 minutes, until softened.

Add the pepper and cook for another minute, then stir in the curry powder, cinnamon and bay leaves and cook for 1 minute.

Pour the boiling water into a heatproof jug, add the stock cube and stir well until dissolved.

Stir the rice into the vegetables in the pan, then add the stock, stir once more and bring to the boil.

Once boiling, turn down the heat, cover with a lid and cook gently for 12 minutes, until the rice is nearly tender – you don't want the liquid to be boiling, just simmering gently so that the rice absorbs the stock.

Meanwhile, bring a pan of water to the boil. Add the eggs and return to a simmer, then cook for 6–8 minutes depending on how runny you like the yolk. Drain, return to the pan and run under cold water until cool enough to handle. Run the eggs against the inside of the pan to crack the shell, then peel the shell off under the water (this is the easiest way to peel eggs).

Stir the peas, lemon zest and juice, half the parsley and plenty of black pepper into the rice and vegetables.

Lay the fish over the top of the rice and cover with a lid. Cook for another 5 minutes until the rice is tender, the stock is fully absorbed and the fish cooked through; it should flake when pressed gently.

Divide between serving plates, cut the eggs into quarters and place on top, with the remaining parsley sprinkled over.

An omelette is such a quick and easy meal to make, yet it can still be healthy and nutritious. Make sure the mushrooms have turned golden brown and released all their liquid before adding them to the beaten eggs and cheese, as you don't want the grey liquid to mix with the egg.

Ultimate Omelette

15g butter
240g mushrooms,
    thickly sliced
6 eggs
135g reduced fat extra
    mature Cheddar cheese,
    grated
low cal oil spray
1 tbsp finely chopped chives
freshly ground black pepper,
    to taste

Heat a non-stick frying pan until hot. Add the butter and mushrooms and fry, stirring, for 3–4 minutes until golden brown and the liquid has evaporated. Remove from the heat and set aside.

Crack the eggs into a bowl and whisk until smooth. Add the grated cheese and cooked mushrooms, season with black pepper and stir until combined.

Return the frying pan to the heat (no need to wash). Add a few squirts of oil spray and one-third of the egg mixture. Roll the pan around so that the egg covers the base, and cook for a couple of minutes until just set.

Tipping the pan up, gently pull the edges of the egg mixture towards the centre, allowing uncooked egg to run over and cook. Repeat until all the egg is just set.

Scatter one-third of the chives over the top, then roll the omelette out of the pan onto a serving plate.

Repeat with the remaining egg mixture and chives to make 2 more omelettes, and serve immediately.

You can add any chopped cooked meats to the mixture along with the cheese. To up the veg content, add some tinned sweetcorn and chopped parsley to the beaten egg mixture, and a little pinch of dried chilli flakes for a touch of spice.

MAKES:
24
PREP TIME:
10 minutes
FREEZING TIME:
1 hour

These are relatively high in sugar, but of the natural kind. When dates and vanilla are blitzed together, they taste particularly delicious, with the vanilla bringing out the sweetness of the dates. Add in some peanut butter and oats and you have a great base for a power bar.

Oat, Date and Nut Power Bars

200g pitted dates, chopped
100g peanut butter
2 tbsp vanilla extract
350g porridge oats
100g dried cranberries
100g cashews, roughly chopped
4 tsp chia seeds

Line a baking tray 23 x 33cm and 3cm deep with baking parchment so that it comes up the sides of the tray.

Tip the dates, peanut butter, vanilla and 175ml water into a food processor and blitz to a coarse purée.

Add the oats and blitz until nearly smooth – it should be smooth enough to stick together when squidged. If it isn't, add a tablespoon more water and blitz again.

Add the cranberries and cashews and pulse until totally combined and holding together.

Transfer the mixture to the lined tray and press it down evenly until flat. Scatter the chia seeds over the top and press them down into the mixture. Place in the freezer for 1 hour to set.

Remove from the freezer and cut into 24 pieces, then decant into a sealable container and store in the fridge for up to 1 week, or in the freezer for 3 months.

Using low fat spread in these oat bars helps keep the saturated fat down, without compromising on the taste. Ground ginger and orange give a fresh, zingy flavour which complements the sweetness of the blueberries.

Blueberry, Oat and Orange Snack Bars

oil, for greasing
300g fine oatmeal
240g low fat spread
200g porridge oats
120g soft light brown sugar
2 tsp ground ginger
finely grated zest and juice
    of 2 oranges
400g fresh or frozen
    blueberries,

Preheat the oven to 180°C/160°C fan/Gas 4. Grease a baking tray 23 x 33cm and 3cm deep with a little oil and line with baking parchment.

Tip the fine oatmeal into a bowl and add the low fat spread. Using your fingertips, rub the mixture together until it forms a breadcrumb-like texture. (Or use a food processor, if you want to speed things up.)

Add the oats, sugar, ginger, orange zest and juice and stir everything together, then add the blueberries and stir once more to combine.

Tip the mixture into the lined tray and press down fairly firmly into an even layer.

Bake in the oven for 40–45 minutes until golden brown and just crispy.

Leave to cool in the tin for 10 minutes before cutting into 24 pieces in the tin. Allow to cool completely before removing and serving, as they will be crumbly until they are cold. They will keep for 3 days at room temperature or up to 3 months in a sealable container in the freezer. To defrost, simply leave at room temperature for 1 hour.

Make a double batch then cover and refrigerate until needed. Transfer 3 at a time to a heatproof plate, cover with kitchen paper and microwave on high for 1 minute until hot through.

SERVES/MAKES:
3/9
PREP TIME:
5 minutes
COOKING TIME:
20 minutes

Pancakes go down well at any time of the day, and using wholemeal flour in these ups the fibre content. Packing them with a portion of mixed berries and serving with a dollop of natural yoghurt makes them a substantial dish.

Fruity Crêpes

150g wholemeal flour
1 egg
300ml semi-skimmed milk
low cal oil spray

TO SERVE
150g low fat natural yoghurt
240g mixed berries

Tip the flour into a bowl and make a well in the centre.

Crack the egg into the well, then pour in the milk and, starting in the centre, whisk very well, moving the whisk out towards the edges to incorporate all the flour. Keep whisking until you have a smooth batter.

Heat a medium non-stick frying pan until hot. Add a squirt of oil spray to the pan, then add a small ladleful of batter (about 3 tablespoons). Lift the pan and swirl the batter around until it covers the base of the pan.

Cook for 1–2 minutes until set all the way across, then run a palette knife around the edge then under the crêpe, and flip it over. Cook for another 45 seconds until lightly coloured, then slide onto a plate.

Repeat with the remaining batter until you have 9 pancakes, spraying the pan with a little oil between each pancake.

Divide the pancakes between 3 serving plates and top with yoghurt and berries, then either roll up or fold into quarters.

You might want to adjust the heat after the first pancake; a good medium to high is normally ok for pancakes – you want them to colour lightly and cook through, not burn!

You don't have to make porridge in a pan, standing and stirring – you can mix in a flash then bake it in the oven. This gives quite firm results, so if you like a softer porridge just add a little more milk.

Baked Spiced Honey and Apple Porridge

2 eating apples,
   halved and cored
160g porridge oats
1 tsp ground cinnamon
1 tsp ground ginger
4 cardamom pods,
   split and seeds crushed
   with the back of a spoon
   or rolling pin
4 tsp chopped mixed nuts
250ml semi-skimmed milk
2 tbsp clear honey

Preheat the oven to 200°C/180° fan/Gas 6.

Grate 1½ of the apples into a bowl (keep the skin on) then add the oats, spices and nuts and mix really well.

Pour the milk into a saucepan, add the honey and heat until just simmering and the honey has dissolved.

Pour the hot milk over the oat mixture, stir well then tip into a medium ovenproof dish.

Thinly slice the remaining half apple and place in a layer over the top of the porridge.

Bake in the oven for 20 minutes until the oats have absorbed all the milk and the apple slices are just golden brown and tender. Serve immediately.

Decant any left over into a sealable container and transfer to the fridge where it will keep for 3 days. To reheat, transfer to a heatproof bowl, cover with kitchen paper and heat in the microwave on high for 2 minutes until piping hot.

The idea of this is that you make the muffin base and divide it in half, then add in a savoury element and a sweet element, and bake them all at the same time. Always allow your muffins to cool for 10 minutes before peeling them out of their paper cases, otherwise they tend to stick to the paper!

Two-way Muffins

175g self-raising flour
100g porridge oats
1 tsp bicarbonate of soda
3 eggs
100ml semi-skimmed milk
75g reduced fat spread,
    melted

FOR THE SAVOURY MUFFINS
1 small/medium courgette
60g reduced fat extra mature
    Cheddar cheese, grated
½ tsp dried thyme
freshly ground black pepper,
    to taste

FOR THE SWEET MUFFINS
2 tbsp clear honey
60g flaked almonds
80g raspberries

Preheat the oven to 190°C/170°C fan/Gas 5. Line a deep 12-hole muffin tin with muffin cases.

For the savoury muffins, coarsely grate the courgette into a tea towel, squeeze over the sink to get rid of any excess water then set aside – you need about 120g.

For the base muffin mixture, tip the flour, oats and bicarbonate of soda into a large bowl and mix until combined.

Crack the eggs into a second bowl, then add the milk and melted spread and mix well until smooth.

Pour the wet mixture onto the dry mixture and stir together until just combined.

Immediately remove half the mixture to the bowl that had the eggs in.

Add the grated courgette to one half, along with the cheese, thyme and black pepper and mix gently – you don't want to overmix. Divide between 6 of the muffin cases.

Add the honey and flaked almonds to the second bowl of mixture and mix lightly, then gently fold in the raspberries. Divide the mixture between the remaining 6 muffin cases.

Bake all the muffins in the oven for 15–18 minutes until golden brown and risen.

Remove and allow to cool in the tin for 10 minutes before removing and serving warm. These will keep for up to 3 days in the fridge. To reheat, simply pop in the microwave on a heatproof plate and heat on high for 30 seconds until hot.

Put together your own ready-to-go porridge pots in 5 minutes – simply mix all the ingredients together then decant into clean jam jars or heatproof sealable containers. You can grab and go in the morning then simply add boiling water.

Apple and Cinnamon Porridge Pots

1 tbsp ground cinnamon
100g dried cranberries
100g dried apple, chopped
100g mixed chopped nuts
100g mixed seeds
250g smooth porridge oats
250g regular rolled oats
175–200ml boiling water
    per serving, according
    to consistency preference

Tip all the ingredients except the oats into a large airtight container and mix together until evenly distributed. Add the oats and mix once more.

Decant 60g (about 4 heaped tablespoons) into a container (clean jam jar or heatproof sealable container), seal and transport to work.

Add the boiling water and stir well, then cover with a lid and leave for 5 minutes before stirring once more and serving immediately. The dry mixture will keep for up to 2 months.

You can add 40g fresh berries, or 50g 0% fat Greek yoghurt per portion. For a creamier consistency, use skimmed milk instead of water. If you prefer it sweeter, add 1 tsp honey.

You can use regular oats in this but will need to blend for longer to get the silky smooth texture that using smooth porridge oats gives you here. Add any berries that you fancy if you haven't got any strawberries to hand.

Oaty Smoothie

90g smooth porridge oats
120g strawberries, hulled and halved
   (about 10 medium strawberries)
2 small bananas, peeled and roughly chopped
300ml skimmed milk, or more to taste

Tip the oats, strawberries and bananas into a blender.

Pour in the milk, adding more if you prefer a runnier smoothie, then blitz until as pink as can be and completely smooth – the longer you blitz it, the more it breaks down the fruit and the more the flavour intensifies.

Divide between serving glasses and serve immediately. Alternatively, place in a sealable container in the fridge, where it will keep for up to 2 days.

Coconut and Orange Granola

This is great served with a little 0% fat Greek yoghurt and topped with some sliced satsumas, or berries. It also makes a really quick crumble-style topping for some cooked fruit.

500g jumbo porridge oats
100g mixed seeds
50g dried cranberries
50g sultanas
50g desiccated coconut
50g flaked almonds
4 tbsp date syrup
4 tbsp rapeseed oil
2 tsp vanilla extract
finely grated zest of
    2 oranges

Preheat the oven to 170°C/150°C fan/Gas 3. Line 2–3 large baking trays with baking parchment.

Tip the oats, seeds, dried cranberries, sultanas, coconut and flaked almonds into a large bowl and mix together.

Tip the date syrup, oil and vanilla extract into a small pan and warm gently, until just melted. Add the orange zest and stir it through.

Drizzle the melted mixture over the oat mixture, then get your hands in and mix really well – you want everything to be coated in oil, as this is what will make it crisp. Divide between the lined trays and wiggle the trays so that the mixture sits in a single, even layer.

Bake in the oven for 10 minutes, then check to see if it is crisping and browning. Stir the mixture around on the trays then return to the oven for another 5 minutes until evenly browned.

Allow to cool to room temperature before decanting into a sealable container, where it will keep for up to 1 month.

Tinned potatoes are an easy addition to these eggs and make it a one-pan dish that ticks all the boxes for flavour, as well as giving you two of your 5-a-day.

One-pan Spicy Eggs

1 tsp olive oil
1 onion, roughly chopped
1 x 300g tin potatoes,
    drained, rinsed and
    roughly chopped
80g button mushrooms,
    halved
1 tsp ground cumin
1 tsp ground coriander
1 tsp smoked paprika
pinch of chilli powder
¼ tsp sea salt
1 x 400g tin chopped
    tomatoes
80g frozen spinach
2 eggs
freshly ground black pepper,
    to taste
2 tsp roughly chopped
    flat-leaf parsley, to serve

Heat a medium non-stick frying pan until hot. Add the oil and onion and cook for 3–4 minutes until just softening.

Add the potatoes, mushrooms, spices and salt and stir-fry for a couple of minutes until starting to colour on the edges.

Add the tomatoes and some black pepper and bring to the boil, then turn down the heat. Add the spinach and simmer for 2–3 minutes, stirring occasionally, until the spinach has softened and the sauce thickened slightly.

Make 2 hollows in the mixture and crack an egg into each. Cover with a lid and simmer for 3–4 minutes until the eggs are cooked to your liking.

Transfer to serving bowls or plates and scatter the parsley over the top.

A twist on chocolate milk, banana helps give a natural sweetness to these overnight oats. Adding cinnamon and vanilla gives an extra boost and complements the banana flavour.

Banana Chocolate Overnight Oats

3 ripe bananas
5 tbsp cocoa powder
1 tbsp ground cinnamon
1 tbsp vanilla extract
500ml semi-skimmed milk
   (or whichever type of milk
   you want to use)
200g porridge oats
200g strawberries, hulled
   and roughly chopped

Peel and chop 2 of the bananas and place in a blender with the cocoa powder, cinnamon, vanilla and milk. Blitz until smooth.

Tip the oats into a large sealable container then add the banana and cocoa mixture and mix really well.

Seal and place in the fridge overnight – the oats will absorb the banana cocoa milk.

Serve in the morning topped with the remaining banana, chopped, and the strawberries.

If you like, top with raspberries, blueberries or blackberries and a handful of seeds.

There's nothing to say that you can't use tinned fruit in a smoothie – just make sure that you're using one in fruit juice not syrup. Tinned peaches and pears go equally well in this smoothie.

Super Green Smoothie

1 avocado, peeled, stoned and roughly chopped
200g frozen spinach
1 x 435g tin pineapple in fruit juice
300ml chilled unsweetened oat milk
1 tbsp vanilla extract

Place all the ingredients in a blender and blitz until totally smooth.

Divide between glasses and serve immediately.

Unsweetened oat milk can be a great alternative to cows' milk in smoothies, and not just for people who are lactose intolerant – it's a source of fibre, low in fat and often comes fortified with vitamins and minerals.

light lunches & snacks

menu

Smoked Mackerel Pâté *71*

Salmon Poke Bowl *72*

Sweetcorn, Pea and Courgette Fritters
 with Poached Egg 74

Roasted Lemon and Onion Butter Bean Houmous
 76

Pick 'n' Mix Fish Parcels
 with Greek Couscous Salad 78

Tuna Niçoise *82*

Spiced Feta and Chickpea Sweet Jacket Potato *85*

Tomato and Bean Soup *86*

Thai Larb Gai Cups *88*

Pizza Toast (Superhero Tomato Sauce) *90*

Ham, Cheese and Vegetable Pancakes *91*

Four-way Chicken Breasts *92*

Leek and Potato Soup
 with Cheese and Onion Bread 94

Speedy Microwave Frittata *98*

Chicken, Spelt and Pepper Salad *101*

This pâté is quick and easy to pull together – somehow, by mashing the mackerel with cream cheese, horseradish and lemon, it becomes a thing of beauty to be enjoyed with a fresh crusty roll and some veg.

Smoked Mackerel Pâté

175g smoked mackerel, skinned
　　and boned
100g lightest cream cheese
1 tsp fresh lemon juice
1 tbsp horseradish sauce
freshly ground black pepper,
　　to taste

TO SERVE
2 carrots, peeled and cut into batons
1 cucumber, cut into batons
2 celery sticks, cut into batons
160g cherry tomatoes
4 crusty rolls

Flake the smoked mackerel into a bowl, add the cream cheese, lemon juice and horseradish and mash together until nearly smooth. Alternatively, place in a food processor and pulse until it forms a rough paste.

Season with black pepper and serve with the veg batons, tomatoes and crusty rolls.

You could use hot smoked salmon or smoked herring instead of mackerel here. The flavours will work just as well as the smoked mackerel. Also, if you like a kick to your pâté, add a small dash of chilli sauce.

Keep any leftovers in the fridge and serve on toast for lunch, or with toasted pitta and a crunchy green salad for a quick supper.

Salmon Poke Bowl

The term 'poke' has its roots in Hawaiian cuisine, and simply means cut into pieces. Traditionally it was made with raw fish, but here hot-smoked salmon makes a great no-cook addition to this flavoursome bowl of noodles and veg.

180g rice noodles
2 spring onions, finely sliced
2 tbsp roughly chopped coriander
80g frozen edamame beans, defrosted
1 tbsp toasted sesame oil
2 tbsp reduced-salt soy sauce
½ tsp dried chilli flakes
finely grated zest and juice of 1 lime

1 avocado, peeled, stoned and roughly chopped
2 red and green peppers, deseeded and cut into thick strips
1 red onion, finely sliced
1 carrot, peeled and sliced into ribbons using a swivel peeler
180g hot-smoked salmon fillets, skinned

Tip the noodles into a large heatproof bowl and pour over enough boiling water to cover. Stir, then leave to soak for at least 5–10 minutes until tender.

Drain the noodles and stir in the spring onions, coriander and half the edamame beans; mix well.

Tip the sesame oil, soy sauce, chilli flakes, lime zest and juice into a small bowl and whisk together. Pour half of it over the noodles and toss to coat, then divide the noodles between 2 serving bowls.

Divide the avocado, peppers, red onion, carrot and remaining edamame beans between the bowls.

Flake the salmon onto the noodles and drizzle with the remaining dressing to serve.

Fritters are a great way of using up leftover veg, supplemented with peas and sweetcorn from the freezer. Serve with a poached egg and you have a quick meal ready in under 20 minutes.

Sweetcorn, Pea and Courgette Fritters *with Poached Egg*

6 eggs
150ml semi-skimmed milk
150g self-raising flour
½ tsp fine sea salt
160g frozen sweetcorn
160g frozen peas
1 courgette, coarsely grated
4 spring onions, roughly
  chopped
2 tsp vegetable oil
1 tbsp white wine vinegar
freshly ground black pepper,
  to taste
1 tbsp finely chopped chives,
  to serve

Crack 2 of the eggs into a large bowl, add the milk, flour, salt and some black pepper and whisk until smooth.

Stir in the sweetcorn, peas, courgette and spring onions and mix well, then whisk once more.

Heat a non-stick frying pan until medium hot. Add a little of the oil then add 4 separate ladlefuls of batter. Turn the heat down to low and cook for 1–2 minutes until you can see bubbles bursting on the surface of each. Flip them over and cook for a further 1–2 minutes until just set.

Lift the fritters out onto a plate and set aside, then repeat with the remaining batter, adding more oil to the pan first.

Meanwhile, fill a pan with water, add the vinegar and heat until just simmering. Crack 2 of the remaining eggs into 2 small cups.

Whisk the centre of the pan to create a vortex and carefully pour the 2 eggs in, one at a time. Cook gently for 2–3 minutes, until the white is set and the yolk still just runny.

Remove with a slotted spoon and drain on kitchen paper, then repeat with the remaining 2 eggs.

Divide the fritters between serving plates, top with a poached egg, a grinding of black pepper and a sprinkling of chives, and serve immediately.

Roasting lemons with cumin- and coriander-coated onions helps turn a humble tin of butter beans into a luxurious-tasting houmous. Great served with some freshly toasted pitta bread.

Roasted Lemon and Onion Butter Bean Houmous

3 tsp olive oil

2 onions, cut into
    thin wedges

1 tbsp ground cumin

1 tbsp ground coriander

2 garlic cloves, finely grated
    or crushed

½ tsp sea salt

1 lemon, cut into thin wedges

2 x 400g tins butter beans,
    drained and rinsed

2 tbsp tahini

freshly ground black pepper,
    to taste

Preheat the oven to 220°C/200°C fan/Gas 7.

Pour 1 teaspoon of the oil into a bowl and add the onions, cumin, coriander, garlic, salt and plenty of black pepper. Toss until the onions are coated in the spice mixture.

Tip out onto a roasting tray then add the lemon wedges around the outside of the onions. Roast in the oven for 30 minutes until both the onions and lemon are tender and just charred around the edges.

Meanwhile, tip the butter beans, remaining 2 teaspoons of oil and the tahini into a food processor. Add two-thirds of the roasted onions along with the flesh from the roasted lemons. Add 4 tablespoons water and blitz until it forms a coarse purée.

Decant into a serving bowl. Finely chop the remaining roasted onions, scatter over the top and serve immediately. This will keep for up to 3 days in an airtight container in the fridge.

A perfect dish for when you have friends or family round, this gives you three different ways to flavour pieces of cod or haddock. Steamed in foil parcels, it's an easy way to cook fish while you make the couscous salad to serve with it.

Pick 'n' Mix Fish Parcels
with Greek Couscous Salad

10 x 150g cod or haddock
    fillets, skinned and pin-
    boned
1 lemon, thinly sliced
1 tbsp roughly chopped dill
1 medium shallot, finely sliced
½ red onion, finely sliced
160g cherry tomatoes,
    halved
40g black pitted olives,
    roughly chopped
1 tbsp roughly chopped
    basil
2 tbsp olive oil
1 tbsp tomato purée
½ tsp dried chilli flakes
½ tsp smoked paprika
finely grated zest and juice
    of ½ lemon

Preheat the oven to 200°C/180°C fan/Gas 6. Prepare 3 large rectangles of foil.

Divide the fish between the centres of the foil pieces (3 pieces on two, 4 on the remaining one), so that they sit snugly side by side.

Lay the lemon slices over one parcel of 3 pieces, then scatter the dill and shallot over the top.

Lay the red onion over the parcel of 4 pieces, then scatter the cherry tomatoes, olives and basil over the top.

Tip the olive oil into a small bowl, then add the tomato purée, chilli flakes, smoked paprika, lemon zest and juice and mix well. Spoon over the remaining parcel of 3 pieces, spreading all over the fish.

Seal each parcel up by scrunching the foil together at the top – if the foil piece is not big enough, simply lay another smaller piece over the top and crimp together at the edges.

Transfer to 2 baking trays and bake in the oven for 15 minutes until the fish is cooked through. To check, open a parcel carefully and insert a knife into the centre of the fish – if the knife is hot through when you remove it, it's cooked; if not, reseal the parcel and cook for another 5 minutes, then check again.

800g wholewheat couscous
1 tbsp dried oregano
juice of 1 lemon
2 tbsp olive oil
1 red onion, roughly chopped
800ml boiling water
1 cucumber, roughly chopped
400g cherry tomatoes,
    halved
3 tbsp roughly chopped
    mint leaves
3 tbsp roughly chopped
    flat-leaf parsley
freshly ground black pepper,
    to taste

While the fish is baking, prepare the couscous salad. Tip the couscous, oregano, lemon juice, oil and red onion into a heatproof bowl and mix really well.

Pour over the boiling water, mix well then cover with clingfilm and set to one side for 10 minutes until the couscous has absorbed the liquid.

Drag a fork through the couscous to fluff it up – it should be like grains of sand. Stir in the cucumber, tomatoes, mint and parsley then season with plenty of black pepper.

Serve the fish parcels at the table for everyone to dive into, together with the couscous salad.

A perfect store-cupboard dish to turn to when you don't fancy cooking, this salad is almost ready in the time it takes to boil and peel the eggs.

Tuna Niçoise

2 eggs

1 x 400g tin butter beans, drained and rinsed

1 x 300g tin small potatoes in water, drained and roughly chopped

2 spring onions, roughly chopped

1 x 200g tin tuna in spring water, drained

1 tsp Dijon mustard

2 tsp white wine vinegar

2 tbsp olive oil

2 tsp capers, roughly chopped

1 tbsp finely chopped chives

1 Little Gem lettuce, leaves separated

freshly ground black pepper, to taste

Bring a small pan of water to the boil. Add the eggs and simmer for 5 minutes until soft-boiled. Drain, run under cold water until cool enough to handle, then peel.

While the eggs are cooking, tip the butter beans, potatoes and spring onions into a bowl and toss together. Add the tuna and toss lightly.

Spoon the mustard, vinegar and olive oil into a bowl and whisk together, then season with black pepper. Stir in the capers and half the chives.

Drizzle the dressing over the salad and toss until just coated.

Divide the lettuce and salad between serving bowls.

Cut the eggs into quarters and place on the salad, then scatter the remaining chives over the top and serve.

This can be made in advance and stored in a sealable container in the fridge for up to 2 days.

Sweet potatoes cooked in the microwave are a perfect, quick lunchtime dish – while they are cooking, you can be preparing the filling of toasted chickpeas, feta and tomato, then all you have to do is pile everything together back under the grill for a couple of minutes to finish.

Spiced Feta and Chickpea Sweet Jacket Potato

2 medium-sized sweet
   potatoes, scrubbed
1 x 400g tin chickpeas,
   drained and rinsed
1½ tsp smoked paprika
1 lemon
100g feta or salad cheese,
   roughly chopped
160g cherry tomatoes,
   halved
freshly ground black pepper,
   to taste
1 tbsp roughly chopped
   flat-leaf parsley, to serve

Pierce each sweet potato with a fork several times, then place on a microwaveable plate. Cover with kitchen paper and microwave on high for 8 minutes. Check they are tender by inserting a knife in the centre – if it goes in easily the potato is ready. If not, return to the microwave for another minute then check once more.

Meanwhile, heat the grill to high.

Tip the chickpeas and smoked paprika onto a baking tray and mix. Zest the lemon over the chickpeas, then cut in half and squeeze over the juice from one half. Season with plenty of black pepper, mix together and place under the grill for 5 minutes, until just beginning to colour and crisp around the edges.

Split the sweet potatoes in half lengthways, spoon the chickpea mixture over the top, then add the feta or salad cheese, and the tomatoes. Return to the grill for 2 minutes until the chickpeas are just crispy and the tomatoes softened, and the cheese turns a little golden at the edges.

Transfer to serving plates, scatter the parsley over the top and serve immediately.

This is a thick and satisfying soup packed full of flavour, vegetables and a good portion of protein too. Make a double batch and keep in the freezer ready to defrost when you feel the need.

Tomato and Bean Soup

1 tsp olive oil
1 onion, roughly chopped
2 celery sticks, roughly chopped
1 carrot, peeled and grated
2 tsp smoked paprika
1 tbsp tomato purée
1 x 400g tin chopped tomatoes
1 x 400g tin cannellini beans, drained and rinsed
½ tsp sea salt
freshly ground black pepper, to taste
1 tbsp roughly chopped basil, to serve

Heat a saucepan until medium hot. Add the oil, onion, celery and carrot and cook for 5 minutes until just softened.

Add the smoked paprika and tomato purée and cook for 1 minute, then tip in the chopped tomatoes and cannellini beans. Half fill the empty tomato tin with water and add to the pan.

Stir well then bring to the boil, turn the heat down and simmer for about 10 minutes until slightly thickened and the vegetables are soft.

Stir in the salt and some black pepper, then use a hand-held stick blender to blitz until smooth.

Transfer to serving bowls and top with a grinding of black pepper and the basil.

Thai Larb Gai Cups

As ever, when cooking a stir fry, be sure to prepare all your ingredients before you even heat the wok, as you will find this dish comes together very quickly. Packed full of flavour, it's a perfect light lunch and a great one to pack up and take with you.

1 tsp vegetable oil
400g chicken mince
1 bunch spring onions, finely sliced
2 garlic cloves, finely grated or crushed
5cm piece of ginger, peeled and grated
2 tsp reduced-salt soy sauce
finely grated zest and juice of 1 lime
1 tbsp roughly chopped coriander
1 tbsp roughly chopped mint
2 Little Gem lettuces, leaves separated
2 red chillies, deseeded and finely chopped, to serve (optional)

Heat a wok or frying pan until hot. Add the oil and chicken mince and stir-fry for 2–3 minutes until just browning.

Add the spring onions, garlic and ginger and stir-fry for 2 minutes, then add the soy sauce and stir-fry for another 2 minutes until the chicken is cooked through and the spring onions are tender.

Remove from the heat and stir in the lime zest and juice, coriander and mint.

Divide the lettuce leaves between serving plates, then spoon the chicken mixture into the leaves. Top with chilli, if you fancy, and eat immediately.

Cooled leftovers will keep in a sealable container in the fridge for 3 days. Eat cold or transfer one portion to a heatproof bowl, cover with kitchen paper and heat on high for 2 minutes until hot through.

MAKES:
1.5kg
PREP TIME:
20 minutes
COOKING TIME:
40 minutes

A batch of this tomato sauce can be turned into many different dishes – a simple tomato pasta, with meat or lentils added to make a bolognaise, or used as the base for a curry, but the easiest and quickest is pizza toast. Spread a little across some toasted bread and add whatever toppings you fancy to make a quick veg-packed pizza.

Superhero Tomato Sauce

1 tbsp olive oil
2 onions, roughly chopped
4 garlic cloves, roughly crushed or
    chopped
2 carrots, peeled and grated
2 celery sticks, roughly chopped
2 red peppers, deseeded
    and roughly chopped
1½ tsp dried mixed herbs
3 tbsp tomato purée
2 x 400g tins chopped tomatoes
1 small bunch basil
½ tsp sea salt
freshly ground black
    pepper, to taste

Heat a large sauté pan or saucepan until hot. Add the olive oil and onions, stir well then cook over a low heat for 5 minutes until just softened.

Add the garlic, carrot, celery and red peppers and stir very well. Cover with a lid and cook for 10 minutes, stirring occasionally, then add the dried mixed herbs and tomato purée and stir once more.

Add the tinned tomatoes and bring to the boil. Pour enough water into one of the empty cans to half fill it, and swirl around. Pour into the second empty can and swirl again, then pour into the pan and stir well.

Turn the heat down to a simmer, cover and cook for 15 minutes until the vegetables are soft.

When the sauce is ready, stir in the basil, salt and black pepper then blitz with a hand-held stick blender or decant in batches to a blender and blitz until smooth.

Divide into sealable containers and allow to cool to room temperature before placing in the fridge or freezer. The sauce will keep for 3 days in the fridge or 1 month in the freezer. Defrost in the fridge overnight before using.

SERVES: 3
PREP TIME: 5 minutes
COOKING TIME: 8 minutes

3 large slices of gluten-free
    wholemeal bread
120g Superhero Tomato Sauce
½ x 125g reduced fat mozzarella,
    roughly chopped
12 slices of pepperoni
45g 50% reduced fat mature Cheddar
    cheese, grated
3 medium carrots, peeled and
    cut into batons
1 small cucumber, cut into batons

Pizza Toast

Preheat the grill to high.

Toast the bread on one side until golden brown, then flip over and toast until the second side just loses its softness but doesn't colour.

Spread the tomato sauce onto the lighter toasted bread side, then top with mozzarella, pepperoni and grated Cheddar.

Return to the grill to cook for 2–3 minutes until golden and bubbling.

Divide between serving plates and serve immediately with the carrots and cucumber.

SERVES/MAKES:
5/12
PREP TIME:
5 minutes
COOKING TIME:
25 minutes

Adding a spoonful of your favourite mustard to these pancakes gives them a savoury slant, making them a perfect match for the simple ham and cheese filling. The peas and tomatoes balance the meal out, providing at least one of your 5-a-day. You can freeze any leftover pancakes for a quick meal from the freezer.

Ham, Cheese and Vegetable Pancakes

400g cherry tomatoes, halved
200g plain flour
2 eggs
400ml semi-skimmed milk
1 tsp mustard
low cal oil spray
125g 50% reduced fat mature
    Cheddar cheese, grated
100g thinly sliced ham, shredded
200g frozen peas, defrosted

Preheat the oven to 200°C/180°C fan/Gas 6 and line a large baking tray with greaseproof paper.

Place the cherry tomatoes cut-side up on a separate oven tray and roast in the oven for 10–15 minutes until just softened.

Meanwhile, tip the flour into a bowl and crack the eggs into the centre. Add the milk, mustard and 100ml water and whisk, starting in the middle and working outwards, until you have a smooth batter.

Heat a non-stick frying pan until hot. Add a couple of sprays of oil, then pour a ladleful of batter into the pan and swirl around, until the base is coated.

Cook for 30–45 seconds until just golden and set, then flip over and cook for another 30–45 seconds until cooked through and golden. Repeat with the remaining batter, adding a couple of sprays of oil for each. Lay the cooked pancakes on a sheet of greaseproof paper in a line as they come out of the pan. You will have 2 spare pancakes, which you can either save for dessert, or freeze for another time.

Scatter a little grated cheese, ham and peas over the top of each pancake. Fold one side over and place on the lined baking tray.

Cook in the oven for 5 minutes until hot through and the cheese has melted. Serve with the roasted cherry tomatoes alongside.

Plain chicken can sometimes become a little boring in your lunchtime sandwiches and wraps, so here are four different ways to liven it up – a dollop of pesto, sprinkle of Cajun spices, sprig of rosemary with a squeeze of lemon and a drizzle of soy and honey. They can all be cooked at the same time, leaving you free to decide which one to eat first!

Four-way Chicken Breasts

4 boneless skinless chicken
  breasts
1 tsp olive oil
pinch of dried rosemary
2 slices of lemon
1 tbsp pesto
1 tsp Cajun seasoning
1 lime, halved
1 tsp reduced-salt soy sauce
1 tsp clear honey

Preheat the oven to 200°C/180°C fan/Gas 6.

Place the chicken breasts on a foil-lined baking tray and drizzle the oil over the top. Toss together until coated then lay each one into a corner of the tray.

On one, scatter the dried rosemary then lay the lemon slices on top. On the next, spread the pesto all over the chicken. Scatter the Cajun seasoning over the top of the next, then squeeze the juice from one lime half over that.

Mix the soy, honey and juice from the remaining lime half together and pour over the last chicken breast.

Cover the tray with foil and roast in the oven for 10 minutes, then remove the foil and roast for another 8–10 minutes until cooked through. To check, pierce the fattest part of the chicken with a sharp knife – if the juices run clear, it is cooked. If not, return to the oven and cook for another 5 minutes and check again.

Transfer the chicken to a sealable container and chill in the fridge until needed, where it will keep for up to 3 days.

SERVES:
6

PREP TIME:
20 minutes

COOKING TIME:
50 minutes

A quick yeast-free bread that's packed full of flavour and ready in under an hour, this makes a great midweek treat to go with a classic leek and potato soup. Slice any leftover bread and layer with parchment paper then pop in a sealed container or bag in the freezer. To reheat, simply toast for a couple of minutes.

Leek and Potato Soup
with Cheese and Onion Bread

FOR THE BREAD

low cal oil spray, for greasing
250g self-raising flour
1 tbsp onion granules
½ tsp sea salt
150g reduced fat mature
    Cheddar cheese,
    coarsely grated
275ml skimmed milk
1 egg
2 tbsp low fat natural yoghurt
freshly ground black pepper,
    to taste

For the bread, preheat the oven to 180°C/160°C fan/Gas 4. Spray a little oil over the insides of a 1kg loaf tin.

Tip the flour, onion granules, salt and grated cheese into a large bowl and mix together, then season with plenty of black pepper.

Make a well in the centre of the mixture and add the milk, egg and yoghurt. Mix really well until combined into a thick batter.

Pour into the greased loaf tin and smooth over the top. Bake in the oven for 45–50 minutes until golden brown and risen. Check that the bread is cooked by inserting a skewer into the centre – if it comes out clean, then it is ready. If not, return to the oven for another 5 minutes and repeat.

Allow to cool in the tin for at least 10 minutes before removing and slicing.

1 tbsp olive oil

1 onion, roughly chopped

2 medium leeks, finely sliced

250g potatoes (1 medium),
   scrubbed and chopped
   into dice about 1cm

1 reduced-salt vegetable
   stock cube

400ml skimmed milk

Meanwhile, for the soup, heat a saucepan until medium hot. Add the oil, onion and leeks, stir well, then cover with a lid and cook over a gentle heat for 4–5 minutes until just softened.

Add the diced potatoes and 400ml water to the pan and bring to the boil.

Crumble the stock cube into the pan then add the milk and return to the boil, stirring occasionally. Turn the heat down and simmer for 5–7 minutes until the veg are all tender.

Blitz until smooth using a hand-held stick blender, then season with black pepper.

Divide between serving bowls and serve with the cheese and onion bread.

Cooled leftover soup will keep in a sealable container in the fridge for up to 3 days. To reheat, transfer to a heatproof bowl, cover with kitchen paper and microwave on high for 2 minutes then stir and check the heat.

This is one step on from microwaved scrambled eggs, making it a meal in one bowl. You can add whatever veg or cooked meat you have in the fridge – try chicken and sweetcorn, or ham and peas. Just be aware that the wider the bowl you use, the faster the eggs will cook, so watch your timings to get it just set in the middle.

Speedy Microwave Frittata

15g butter
6 eggs
240g cherry tomatoes,
   halved
100g feta or salad cheese,
   roughly chopped
1 tbsp flat-leaf parsley,
   roughly chopped
freshly ground black pepper,
   to taste

Melt the butter in a heatproof mixing bowl for a few seconds in the microwave (to prevent the eggs from sticking).

Crack the eggs into the melted butter and whisk until just broken up.

Add the cherry tomatoes, feta or salad cheese and parsley, season well with black pepper then whisk once more.

Place in the microwave and heat on high for 5 minutes – the eggs should be puffed up and set, but not rock solid. If the eggs are not set, return to the microwave and cook for another 60 seconds, then check again.

Tip onto a plate and serve.

This will keep for 2 days in the fridge and is a great one to pack up and take for lunch the next day.

SERVES:
2
PREP TIME:
10 minutes
COOKING TIME:
25 minutes

Spelt is a type of wheat grain with a lovely nutty flavour and chewy texture. Cooked with some spices, it makes a great base for a chicken salad and works really well as the base in the Smoked Fish Burgers (see page 91).

Chicken, Spelt and Pepper Salad

2 tbsp olive oil
1 tbsp ground cumin
1 tbsp ground coriander
300g spelt
1 litre boiling water
1 reduced-salt chicken stock
   cube, crumbled
40g kale, roughly chopped
½ yellow or red pepper, deseeded
   and roughly chopped
1 small roast chicken breast
   (see page 92), sliced or torn
   into strips
80g cucumber (about ¼),
   roughly chopped
1 tbsp pine nuts, toasted
1 tbsp roughly chopped basil
1 tsp fresh lemon juice
1 tbsp balsamic vinegar
2 tbsp Greek yoghurt
pinch of sea salt
freshly ground black pepper,
   to taste

Heat a sauté pan or saucepan until medium hot. Add 1 tablespoon of the olive oil, the cumin and coriander, and fry for 30 seconds.

Add the spelt and boiling water and bring to the boil. Stir in the crumbled stock cube and simmer for 15–20 minutes until just tender.

Drain off the excess liquid. (If not using immediately, decant into a sealable container and cool to room temperature before transferring to the fridge, where it will keep for 3 days.) Leave 100g spelt (2 portions) in the pan and stir in the kale and pepper. Cover with a lid and steam for another 5 minutes until the kale and pepper are just tender. Season with black pepper then transfer to a serving dish.

Pile the chicken and cucumber on top and scatter the pine nuts and basil over the top.

Put the lemon juice in a small bowl, add the vinegar, remaining tablespoon of olive oil, yoghurt, salt and black pepper and whisk together until thickened. Spoon over the salad to serve.

easy
veggie

menu

A great veggie alternative to chicken nuggets, you can make these with the kids and let them choose which flavourings to add to the breadcrumbs. Go as spicy as you like, or stick to lemon zest.

Veggie 'Nuggets'
with Roasted Garlic Dip

1 medium/large sweet potato, peeled and cut in half lengthways, then into 1cm thick slices
160g baby corn, cut in half if long
160g broccoli (about ⅓ head), cut into evenly sized florets
2 peppers (any colour), deseeded and thickly sliced
4 tbsp plain flour
4 eggs
¼ tsp fine sea salt
¾ tsp freshly ground black pepper, plus extra for the dip
50g panko breadcrumbs
variety of dried seasonings – dried chilli flakes / smoked paprika / dried parsley
finely grated zest of 1 lemon
2 tbsp onion powder

FOR THE ROASTED GARLIC DIP
1 whole garlic bulb
300g 0% fat Greek yoghurt
2 tbsp roughly chopped parsley leaves

Preheat the oven to 210°C/190°C fan/Gas 7 and line 2 baking trays with baking parchment or foil.

Wrap the garlic bulb in foil and bake in the oven for 25 minutes. Remove and set aside.

Meanwhile, tip all the vegetables into a bowl, sprinkle with the flour and toss together until lightly coated.

Crack the eggs into a shallow bowl, season with the salt and pepper, then beat until smooth.

Tip the breadcrumbs into a medium bowl and add your dried seasoning/s of choice, the lemon zest and onion powder. Mix to combine.

Using one hand, drop a few pieces of the floured vegetables at a time the beaten egg and toss until totally coated.

Drop the eggy pieces into the flavoured breadcrumbs using the same hand then, using your clean hand, toss again until totally coated. Lay onto the lined baking trays in a single layer. Repeat with the remaining vegetables, egg and breadcrumbs.

Bake in the oven for 20–25 minutes until golden brown, crunchy on the outside and just tender inside. To check that they are tender, pierce with the tip of a knife: if the nugget slides off the knife, the veg are tender. If not, return to the oven for another 5 minutes – it does depend how big your florets are!

While the nuggets are baking, tip the yoghurt into a bowl. Cut the ends off of the roasted garlic cloves and squeeze as much as you like into the yoghurt. Add the parsley, season with black pepper and beat well to combine.

Serve the nuggets with the garlic dip alongside.

Including leeks in the tomato sauce makes this pasta bake beautifully sweet and ups the vegetable content. If making for later, just run the pasta under cold water to cool before tossing with the sauce – you can then place in the fridge for up to 3 days, before popping in the oven and heating for 25 minutes until bubbling.

Broccoli Pasta Bake

450g dried fusilli pasta

240g broccoli (about 1 small head), cut into small florets, stems cut into slices 1cm thick

1 tsp olive oil

1 onion, roughly chopped

2 leeks, roughly chopped

2 garlic cloves, finely grated

1 tbsp tomato purée

2 x 400g tins chopped tomatoes

½ tsp salt

2 tbsp natural dried breadcrumbs

60g reduced fat mature Cheddar cheese, grated

freshly ground black pepper, to taste

Preheat the oven to 200°C/180°C fan/Gas 6.

Cook the pasta in a large pan of boiling, salted water for 10 minutes, until just tender but not completely, then add the broccoli and cook for a further 3 minutes until both are tender. Drain into a colander, then immediately place over the empty pan to catch some of the cooking water.

While the pasta is cooking, heat a sauté pan until hot. Add the oil, onion and leeks and cook for 2 minutes until just softening.

Add the garlic and cook for 1 minute, then add the tomato purée and cook for another minute.

Add the tinned tomatoes and bring to the boil. Turn down the heat and simmer for 5 minutes until thickened and the vegetables are tender. Add the salt and black pepper to taste.

Add the pasta and any water in the pan to the sauce and toss together until coated, then tip into a medium baking dish.

Toss the breadcrumbs and grated cheese together in a small bowl and sprinkle over the top of the pasta. Bake in the oven for 10 minutes, until golden and bubbling on top.

Allow any leftovers to cool to room temperature before covering and storing in the fridge for up to 3 days. To reheat, transfer a portion to a heatproof bowl, cover with kitchen paper and microwave until piping hot.

The chestnut mushrooms and lentils give this vegetarian pie a really meaty feel. If you don't like mustard, you can add a couple of tablespoons of tomato purée in its place, and the topping can be whichever root veg you have to hand, or find lurking at the bottom of the fridge – parsnips, carrots and uncooked beetroot all work equally well.

Mushroom and Lentil Pie

300g small white potatoes, scrubbed
300g swede, peeled and cut into chunks the same size as the potatoes
1 tsp olive oil
1 onion, roughly chopped
400g chestnut mushrooms, thickly sliced
2 garlic cloves, finely grated or crushed
3 tbsp grainy mustard
50ml whipping cream
1 x 400g tin green lentils, drained and rinsed
160g baby spinach leaves
¼ tsp sea salt
freshly grated nutmeg, to taste
50g reduced fat extra mature Cheddar cheese, grated
freshly ground black pepper, to taste

Preheat the grill to medium.

Put the potatoes and swede into a medium saucepan and cover with cold water. Bring to the boil, then turn the heat down and simmer for 15 minutes until just tender. Drain, return to the pan and set aside until cool enough to handle.

Meanwhile, heat a sauté pan until hot. Add the oil and onion and cook over a medium heat for 3–4 minutes until softened.

Add the mushrooms and stir-fry for 2–3 minutes until just colouring and the liquid is evaporating. Stir in the garlic and cook for another minute.

Add 2 tablespoons of the mustard, the cream and lentils to the mushrooms, and bring to the boil. Scatter the spinach over the top then cover with a lid and leave to steam for 2–3 minutes until the spinach has wilted. Stir well then season with black pepper and transfer to 4 individual ovenproof dishes, or one large.

Coarsely grate the potato and swede back into the saucepan. Add the remaining tablespoon of mustard, the salt, some nutmeg and black pepper and half the grated cheese, and mix once more.

Divide the potato mixture between the dishes, piling it loosely on top of the mushroom mixture, then sprinkle the remaining cheese over the top.

Place under the grill for 4–5 minutes until the cheese has melted and the top is golden brown, then serve.

SERVES:
4
PREP TIME:
10 minutes
COOKING TIME:
20 minutes

Adzuki beans and soya pieces provide the protein here, simmered in a flavoursome BBQ-style sauce and served with sour cream and jalapeño chillies. You can use whichever tinned beans you have to hand if you don't have adzuki.

Veggie BBQ Chilli
with Rice

1 tsp vegetable oil
1 onion, roughly chopped
2 garlic cloves, finely grated
   or crushed
2 tsp ground cumin
2 tsp ground coriander
½ tsp smoked paprika
1 tbsp tomato purée
240g soya pieces
60g reduced-salt and -sugar
   brown sauce
200ml apple juice
2 tsp clear honey
1 x 200g tin chopped
   tomatoes
1 x 400g tin adzuki beans,
   drained and rinsed
300g long grain rice
1 x 325g tin sweetcorn
   in water, drained
2 tbsp roughly chopped
   coriander
4 tsp half fat sour cream
1–2 tbsp sliced green jalapeño
   chillies, to taste (optional)

Heat a large sauté pan or saucepan until hot, add the oil and onion and fry for 2–3 minutes until just softened.

Stir in the garlic, cumin, coriander and smoked paprika and fry for 1 minute, then add the tomato purée and stir well.

Add the soya pieces and stir until coated in the onion mixture. Add the brown sauce, apple juice, honey, tomatoes and adzuki beans and stir well, then bring to the boil. Reduce the heat, cover and simmer for 15 minutes, stirring occasionally, until the sauce has thickened and the soya pieces have taken on the flavour of the spices.

Meanwhile, bring a pan of water to the boil. Add the rice and stir well, then bring to the boil. Reduce the heat and simmer for 12–15 minutes until tender, then drain and divide between serving plates.

Stir the sweetcorn and half the coriander into the chilli and simmer for 1 minute until hot, then spoon alongside the rice. Add a teaspoon of sour cream to each serving, the remaining coriander and chillies, if using, and serve immediately.

Transfer any leftover chilli to a sealable container and allow to cool to room temperature, then transfer to the fridge where it will keep for up to 3 days. To reheat, either return to a pan and heat through on the hob until piping hot, or transfer to a heatproof plate, cover with kitchen paper and microwave on high for 3 minutes until hot through.

SERVES:
4 (pesto serves 10)
PREP TIME:
5 minutes
COOKING TIME:
12 minutes

Adding chickpeas to this classic pesto gives an extra boost of both protein and vegetables, as well as bulking it out to stretch much further.

Chickpea and Basil Pesto Pasta

300g dried pasta

1 x 400g tin chickpeas, drained and liquid reserved

1 large bunch basil (100g), stalks included, roughly chopped

4 garlic cloves, roughly chopped

50g Parmesan cheese, grated

2 tbsp extra-virgin olive oil

freshly ground black pepper, to taste

Cook the pasta in a pan of boiling, salted water for 10–12 minutes until tender, according to the packet instructions, then drain and tip back into the pan.

While the pasta is cooking, add the chickpeas (without their liquid) to a food processor and blitz until they are roughly chopped.

Add the basil, garlic, Parmesan, oil and about 6 tablespoons of the chickpea liquid and blitz until as smooth as possible – if necessary, add another 2 tablespoons of chickpea liquid.

Add 200g (50g per person) pesto to the just-drained pasta and mix well until the pasta is coated. Transfer the remaining pesto to a sealable container in the fridge, where it will keep for up to 3 days.

Serve immediately, with a grinding of black pepper over the top.

Rainbow Root Chips

Carrots, parsnips and beetroot all take a similar time to roast when cut into batons. They're perfect paired with any roasted meats, particularly the Honeyed Pork with Apples (see page 150).

400g carrots, peeled and cut into batons 1cm thick
400g parsnips, peeled and cut into batons 1cm thick
400g uncooked beetroot, scrubbed and cut into batons 1cm thick
1 tbsp vegetable oil

2 tsp chopped fresh thyme leaves
2 garlic cloves, finely grated or crushed
freshly ground black pepper, to taste

Preheat the oven to 200°C/180°C fan/Gas 6 and line a large baking tray with baking parchment.

Toss the carrots, parsnips and beetroot onto the tray, drizzle over the oil then toss together so the veg are totally coated.

Spread them out in an even layer and season with black pepper, the thyme and garlic, then toss once more to evenly coat, and spread out in an even layer.

Roast in the oven for 15 minutes, then remove the tray, turn the veg over and return to the oven to roast for a further 15 minutes, until golden and tender.

Colourful Crispy Fries

A dusting of oil and spiced cornflour helps crisp up these fries – just make sure you divide them between 2 trays so there is plenty of space for the air to circulate around as they bake.

2 tbsp cornflour
2 tsp smoked paprika
¼ tsp fine sea salt
2 medium potatoes, scrubbed and cut lengthways into slices 1cm thick
3 medium carrots, peeled and cut lengthways into slices 1cm thick
2 medium-sized sweet potatoes, scrubbed and cut lengthways into slices 1cm thick
2 tbsp vegetable oil

Preheat the oven to 220°C/200°C fan/Gas 7 and line 2 large baking trays with baking parchment.

Tip the cornflour, smoked paprika and salt into a large bowl, then add the vegetables and toss really well until completely coated.

Add the oil and massage in so that the cornflour is coated in the oil, then divide between the 2 baking trays. You don't want them to be crowded; they need to have space around each piece.

Roast in the oven for 20–25 minutes until golden, tender inside and crispy on the outside.

Allow any leftovers to cool to room temperature then decant into
a sealable container and transfer to the fridge where they will
keep for up to 3 days. Eat cold or transfer one portion at a time
to a heatproof bowl, cover with kitchen paper and microwave
on high for 3 minutes until piping hot.

Smoked tofu has so much more flavour than regular tofu, meaning it pairs really well with the home-made teriyaki sauce. Served alongside the roasted vegetables, it makes a substantial meal.

Teriyaki Roasted Vegetables and Tofu

225g smoked tofu, cut into about 2cm cubes
160g broccoli, cut into florets, stems thickly sliced
160g butternut squash, peeled and cut into slices 1cm thick
2 red onions, cut into wedges
100ml (6–7 tbsp) home-made Teriyaki Sauce (see page 140)
80g kale, roughly chopped
2 spring onions, finely sliced, to serve

Preheat the oven to 200°C/180°C fan/Gas 6. Line 2 roasting trays with baking parchment (the mixture gets sticky and you don't want it stuck to the tray).

Tip the tofu onto one tray and the vegetables onto the other.

Place the vegetable tray in the oven to roast for 15 minutes, then remove. Add three-quarters of the teriyaki sauce and the kale and toss the vegetables together.

Drizzle the remaining teriyaki sauce over the tofu and toss to coat, then place both trays in the oven for 10 minutes. The vegetables should be slightly charred around the edges and tender, and the tofu slightly crispy.

Serve immediately, topped with the spring onions.

SERVES:
6
PREP TIME:
10 minutes
COOKING TIME:
40 minutes

A perfect dish to pop in a packed lunch, this is a great big pasta cake, full of flavour and vegetables. Just remember to line the pan with baking parchment so that it slides out easily.

Courgette, Basil and Pasta Slice

300g dried spaghetti
2 medium courgettes, spiralised or coarsely grated
2 tsp olive oil
1 aubergine, roughly chopped
1 onion, roughly chopped
3 garlic cloves, finely grated or crushed
1 tsp dried thyme
2 tbsp tomato purée
2 x 400g tins chopped tomatoes
2 tbsp roughly chopped basil
2 eggs
150g reduced fat mature Cheddar cheese, grated
freshly ground black pepper, to taste

Preheat the oven to 200°C/180°C fan/Gas 6.

Cook the spaghetti in a large pan of boiling, salted water for 8–9 minutes until just tender, then add the courgette and simmer for 2 minutes. Drain into a colander and set aside. (You don't want to overcook either the pasta or courgette as they will cook further in the sauce.)

Meanwhile, heat a large ovenproof sauté pan over a medium heat. Add the oil and aubergine, stir well and fry for 2–3 minutes until just beginning to colour.

Add the onion and cook for 2 minutes then stir in the garlic, thyme and tomato purée and cook for 1 minute. Add the tinned tomatoes and mix really well.

Bring to the boil, then reduce the heat, cover and simmer for 5 minutes until the sauce has reduced slightly. Stir in the basil and season well with black pepper.

Crack the eggs into large bowl, add two-thirds of the grated cheese and plenty of black pepper and whisk together to combine. Add the drained pasta and courgette and mix until totally combined – you need to do this fairly quickly and evenly as you don't want the eggs to curdle. Finally, stir in the tomato sauce.

Wipe out the ovenproof sauté pan, then line it with a large piece of baking parchment (just bigger than the pan) – this just helps remove the cake at the end.

Pour the tomato spaghetti mixture into the pan and press it down into an even layer. Scatter the remaining cheese over the top and bake in the oven for 25 minutes until golden brown and just set.

Ideally leave to cool before slicing, as it will set as it cools. Cut into wedges and serve warm or cold. It will keep in a sealable container in the fridge for up to 3 days. If not serving cold, cover with kitchen paper and heat in the microwave on high for 2 minutes until piping hot.

At first glance this might be a simple pesto pasta, but in fact it's packed full of veggies – leeks, kale and peas are blended together with mature Cheddar cheese to create a purée that coats the pasta.

Hidden Greens Pasta

375g dried pasta
2 medium leeks (about 400g), roughly chopped
100g kale, roughly chopped
200g frozen peas
¼ tsp sea salt
50g reduced fat mature Cheddar cheese, grated
freshly ground black pepper, to taste

Cook the pasta in a pan of boiling, salted water, according to the packet instructions, then drain into a colander, setting the colander back over the pan to catch a little bit of the cooking water.

While the pasta is cooking, add the leeks and kale to a separate pan of boiling water and return to the boil. Turn the heat down and simmer for 3–4 minutes until just tender.

Add the peas, return to the boil and simmer for 1 minute, then drain all the veg, reserving a little of the cooking water. Tip into a blender with the reserved water, add the salt and nearly all the cheese and blitz to a fine purée. Season with black pepper and blitz once more.

Tip the drained pasta and veg purée back into the pasta pan and return to the heat. Cook for 1–2 minutes, stirring constantly, until the pasta is totally coated in sauce and hot through.

Divide between serving plates and top with the remaining cheese and a little black pepper.

You can add any green veg to this – beans, broccoli, spinach. Just make sure that you put the hardest ones in first so that they all end up cooked at the same time.

Grated courgette makes a great 'no-meatball' when bound together with breadcrumbs, egg and cheese. Make sure that you squeeze out as much liquid as possible from the courgette before adding the other ingredients – you'll be amazed at how much liquid there is in a grated courgette!

No-Meatballs and Spaghetti

3 medium courgettes
2 garlic cloves, finely grated
100g fresh breadcrumbs
1 egg
80g reduced fat mature
    Cheddar cheese, grated
2 tsp olive oil
1 onion, roughly chopped
1 tbsp tomato purée
1 x 400g tin chopped
    tomatoes
2 tbsp roughly chopped
    basil
300g dried spaghetti
freshly ground black pepper,
    to taste

Preheat the oven to 200°C/180°C/Gas 6.

Coarsely grate the courgettes into a clean tea towel set over a bowl. Pick the tea towel up and squeeze out the excess moisture from the courgette. Discard the liquid.

Tip the courgette into the bowl, then add the garlic, breadcrumbs, egg, plenty of black pepper and the cheese.

Using your hands, mix everything together until evenly combined. Divide the mixture in half, then in half again. Divide each quarter into 4 so that you have 16 even-sized pieces in total. Roll each piece into a ball, arrange on a roasting tray and roast in the oven for 20 minutes.

Meanwhile, heat a sauté pan or saucepan until medium hot. Add the oil and onion and cook for 3–4 minutes until just softened. Stir in the tomato purée and cook for 1 minute then add the tinned tomatoes and half the basil. Bring to the boil, then turn the heat down and simmer for 15 minutes.

While the sauce and meatballs are cooking, cook the spaghetti in a pan of boiling, salted water until tender, according to the packet instructions. Drain into a colander then immediately place the colander back over the saucepan to catch some of the cooking water.

Toss the spaghetti and cooking water in the pan into the tomato sauce and mix well. Add the courgette balls and toss very gently until just coated in the sauce.

Serve immediately, with the remaining basil scattered over the top.

Topped with quick-pickled red onion, this is a flavour-packed pilau full of vegetables, with the lentils providing both protein and another of your 5-a-day. Great as a main course or an accompaniment to a simple piece of fish or chicken.

Cauliflower Vegetable Pilau

1 red onion, finely sliced

juice of 1 lemon

1 tsp olive oil

1 onion, roughly chopped

2 garlic cloves, crushed
    or finely grated

1 tbsp ground cumin

1 tbsp ground coriander

2 tsp garam masala

1 cauliflower, coarsely grated

2 peppers (any colour),
    deseeded and roughly
    chopped

2 carrots, peeled and grated

1 medium courgette, coarsely
    grated

1 reduced-salt vegetable
    stock cube

2 bay leaves

160g frozen or drained tinned
    sweetcorn in water

2 x 400g tin lentils, drained
    and rinsed

½ tsp sea salt

2 tbsp roughly chopped
    flat-leaf parsley

2 tbsp 0% fat natural yoghurt

freshly ground black pepper,
    to taste

Tip the sliced red onion into a large, clean jam jar and pour the lemon juice over the onion. Seal with the lid and give it a gentle shake – the onion should wilt slightly and be totally covered with the lemon juice. Set aside to pickle.

Meanwhile, heat a sauté pan until hot. Add the oil and chopped onion and cook over a medium heat for 3–4 minutes until softened.

Add the garlic, cumin, coriander and garam masala and cook for 1 minute before stirring in the grated cauliflower. Add the peppers and stir-fry for 2 minutes, then stir in the grated carrots and courgette.

Crumble the stock cube into the pan, then add 500ml water and the bay leaves. Stir well and bring to the boil, then reduce the heat and simmer for 4–5 minutes until the cauliflower and peppers are just tender.

Stir in the sweetcorn and lentils and cook for another 2–3 minutes until hot through.

Season with the salt and plenty of black pepper and stir in three-quarters of the parsley.

Divide between serving plates, top with a dollop of yoghurt, the pickled red onions and remaining parsley, and serve.

It might seem like there are a lot of spices in this, but they are all key spices that work well in your store cupboard in so many ways. You can put them together in many different combinations to make a Middle Eastern dish, Indian dish or simply added to a cake or bake.

Aubergine and Chickpea Tagine *with Citrus Couscous*

1 tbsp olive oil
1 large onion, roughly chopped
2 garlic cloves, finely chopped or
    grated
1 tsp ground cumin
1 tsp ground coriander
1 tsp ground ginger
1 tsp ground cinnamon
2 aubergines, roughly chopped
    (about 2cm pieces)
1 x 400g tin chopped tomatoes
1 reduced-salt vegetable stock cube
1 x 400g tin chickpeas, drained
    and rinsed
80g dried apricots, sliced
1 tbsp honey
4 tbsp roughly chopped coriander

FOR THE CITRUS COUSCOUS
320g couscous
¼ tsp fine sea salt
finely grated zest and juice
    of 1 orange
finely grated zest and juice
    of 1 lemon
1 red onion, finely chopped
freshly ground black pepper,
    to taste

Heat a large sauté pan until hot. Add the olive oil and onion and cook over a medium heat for 3–4 minutes until softened.

Add the garlic and ground spices, stir well then cook for 1 minute.

Stir the aubergines into the spiced onion and fry for another 2 minutes until just coloured. Add the chopped tomatoes then refill the empty can with water and add to the pan with the stock cube, crumbling it in. Bring to the boil, stir in the chickpeas, apricots and honey, then turn the heat down and simmer, uncovered, for 10 minutes. Stir well then cover with a lid and cook for another 5 minutes until the aubergine is tender and the liquid reduced slightly.

Meanwhile, tip the couscous into a large bowl. Add the salt, plenty of black pepper, the orange and lemon zest and juice and the red onion, and stir well. Pour 350ml boiling water over the top and stir really well. Cover the bowl with clingfilm and set aside for 5–10 minutes to allow the couscous to absorb the liquid. Drag a fork through the couscous to separate the grains.

Stir half the coriander into the tagine and the rest into the couscous, then divide between serving bowls.

This pasty uses a quick-flavoured soft dough in place of pastry to encase the filling. Sweet potatoes, leeks and cheese form a chunky filling that steam-cooks in the dough, meaning it's the pasty equivalent of one-pot cooking!

Veggie Cheats Pasties

300g self-raising flour,
   plus extra for dusting
½ tsp fine sea salt
1 tsp mustard powder
1 tsp dried mixed herbs
180g Greek yoghurt
2 medium-sized sweet potatoes
   (about 400g), peeled and
   cut into 1cm chunks
1 large leek (about 200g),
   thinly sliced
175g 50% reduced fat mature
   Cheddar cheese, coarsely
   grated
1 egg, beaten
freshly ground black pepper,
   to taste

Preheat the oven to 200°C/180°C fan/Gas 6 and line 2 medium baking trays with baking parchment.

Tip the flour into a large bowl, add the salt, mustard powder and dried mixed herbs and mix well. Make a well in the centre and spoon the yoghurt into it, then add 5 tablespoons of cold water and stir everything together with a spoon to form a rough dough. Tip out onto a lightly floured work surface and knead for 1–2 minutes until smooth.

Divide the dough into 5 even portions, then roll each piece into a ball. Flatten each ball gently with the palm of your hand, then roll out on a lightly floured surface to disc about 3mm thick and 18cm in diameter.

Tip the sweet potatoes, leeks and grated cheese into a bowl. Season well with plenty of black pepper then add 2 tablespoons water and mix well.

Place the dough discs on a work surface and brush around the edges with the beaten egg. Spoon the vegetable mixture onto the centre of the discs, leaving a good 2cm clear border around the edge. (Tip: keep the bowl of sweet potato mixture on a set of digital scales and set to zero – take 150g out each time per pasty.)

Gently pick up either side of the pastry and pull together to join at the top. Press the edges together to seal and crimp all the way along, making sure they are properly sealed as the vegetables will steam inside the pastry.

Place on the lined trays and brush all over with the beaten egg. Bake in the oven for 15 minutes, then turn the oven temperature down to 180°C/160°C fan/Gas 4 and bake for another 10 minutes until the pastry is golden brown and crispy.

Serve hot, warm or cold.

speedy suppers

menu

Fish Tacos *with Mango Salsa* *131*

Easy Margherita Cheat-zza *132*

Hidden Veg, Salmon and Pea Risotto *135*

Quick Chicken Tikka *with Roti* *136*

Super-speedy Fish Pie *137*

Quick-cook Dahl *138*

Teriyaki Beef Stir Fry *140*

Home-made Fish and Chips *144*

No-waste Calzone *147*

Fish Gumbo *with Pumpkin Seed Pesto* *149*

Honeyed Pork *with Apples* *150*

Spicy Rice with Ham *152*

Mini Gluten- and Lacto-free Toads in the Hole *154*

Broccoli Carbonara *with Speedy Garlic Dough Balls*
  155

Grabbing the fish from the freezer and setting on a covered plate in the fridge in the morning means you can pull these tacos together for a midweek supper in no time at all. You can also use frozen mango for the salsa.

Fish Tacos
with Mango Salsa

1 tsp mild chilli powder
1 tsp ground coriander
1 tsp ground cumin
2 tsp vegetable oil
4 x 90g frozen cod fillets,
    defrosted
4 medium corn tortillas
4 tbsp 0% fat Greek yoghurt
8 coriander sprigs
1 red pepper, deseeded
    and finely sliced

FOR THE MANGO SALSA

1 large mango, peeled, stoned
    and finely chopped
2 spring onions, finely chopped
2 tbsp mint leaves, roughly chopped
finely grated zest and juice
    of 1 lime
2 tbsp roughly chopped coriander
freshly ground black pepper,
    to taste

Preheat the oven to 200°C/180°C fan/Gas 6.

Tip the chilli powder, ground coriander and cumin onto a plate and mix. Drizzle the oil over the cod fillets and toss until coated.

Press the cod into the spices until totally coated, then place on a baking tray. Bake in the oven for 10–15 minutes until cooked through.

Meanwhile, put the mango, spring onions, mint, lime zest and juice and coriander into a bowl and mix until combined. Season with black pepper.

Divide the tortillas between serving plates. Spread yoghurt over each tortilla, then top with the coriander sprigs and red pepper. Flake the cod over the top. Spoon the mango salsa alongside to serve.

SERVES:
4
PREP TIME:
20 minutes
COOKING TIME:
20 minutes

A no-prove dough means that this can be ready in around 30 minutes; just make sure that you have the oven up as high as it will go and place the baking trays in upside down to start with – these act as pizza stones and mean the pizzas will cook quickly.

Easy Margherita Cheat-zza

FOR THE DOUGH

375g self-raising flour,
    plus extra for dusting
75g fine polenta,
    plus extra for dusting
½ tsp sea salt
3 tbsp roughly chopped basil
300g natural yoghurt

FOR THE TOPPING

250ml tomato passata
1 tbsp tomato purée
1 tbsp onion granules
½ tsp dried oregano
100g reduced fat mozzarella,
    torn into pieces
75g reduced fat mature
    Cheddar cheese, grated
freshly ground black pepper,
    to taste

**EXTRA TOPPINGS
(MIX-AND-MATCH
SUGGESTIONS)**

2 peppers (any colour),
    deseeded and sliced
1 red onion, sliced
120g roughly chopped kale
60g pitted green olives

Preheat the oven to as high as it will go.

Place 3 large upturned baking trays in the oven to heat – one on each shelf. If you don't have 3 shelves and you have a cake rack that fits in your oven, you can place that on the oven bottom to use as an additional shelf.

Tip the flour and polenta into a large bowl, add the salt, basil and plenty of black pepper, and combine thoroughly.

Add the yoghurt and 75ml water and mix to a rough dough. Dust the work surface with some flour and polenta, tip the dough out and knead lightly until just smooth.

Divide the dough into 4 and roll each piece into a ball. Using a rolling pin, roll each ball out to around 5mm thick – it doesn't matter what shape! If you like a thicker pizza crust, roll it slightly thicker. Place each piece of rolled-out dough on its own sheet of baking parchment and set aside.

For the sauce, tip the passata into a bowl, add the purée, onion granules, dried oregano and black pepper and mix until combined.

Spoon the mixture over the pizza bases, leaving a clear border of about 1cm around the outside. Sprinkle over half the cheeses then add whichever extra toppings you fancy. Sprinkle the remaining cheese on top.

Open the oven door and slide out one rack at a time, with an upturned baking tray on it. One at a time, pick up a sheet of parchment paper with a pizza on it and place it directly on the hot tray. Repeat with the other pizzas and bake for 10–12 minutes until just crispy around the edges.

Slide onto serving boards and cut into wedges. Serve immediately with extra black pepper.

Using half rice and half cauliflower keeps the carb level down here and ups the amount of veg without compromising on the flavour and texture of the risotto. Cutting the salmon into small cubes helps it cook quickly, making it a one-pan meal.

Hidden Veg, Salmon and Pea Risotto

900ml boiling water
1 reduced salt vegetable stock cube
1 tsp vegetable oil
1 onion, finely chopped
2 garlic cloves, finely grated or crushed
1 tbsp fresh thyme leaves
200g risotto rice
250g cauliflower (½ medium), coarsely grated
200g boneless and skinless salmon fillet, cut into small cubes
160g frozen peas
40g Parmesan cheese, finely grated
2 tbsp roughly chopped flat-leaf parsley
freshly ground black pepper, to taste

Pour the boiling water into a heatproof jug, add the stock cube and stir well until dissolved.

Heat a sauté pan until medium hot, add the oil and onion and sweat for 3–4 minutes until just softening. Add the garlic and thyme and cook for 1 minute.

Add the rice and stir it through the onion. Add a quarter of the stock, stir the rice really well then lower the heat and cook for 5 minutes until the liquid has been absorbed. Repeat this, using a third of the remaining stock, and cook for another 5 minutes.

Tip in the grated cauliflower and remaining stock, stir well and cook over a gentle heat for 5–10 minutes, until all the stock has been absorbed and the rice and cauliflower are just tender.

Stir in the salmon and cook for 2 minutes, then add the peas and cook for another 2 minutes until the salmon is cooked through and the peas are hot.

Add half the grated cheese and parsley and season with black pepper. Divide the risotto between serving bowls and top with the remaining cheese and parsley to serve.

Boneless skinless chicken thighs are really versatile and can take on strong flavours. Here they cook in the tikka sauce while the roti are rolled and fried. There's nothing better than a freshly cooked roti to go with a curry!

Quick Chicken Tikka
with Roti

1 tbsp vegetable oil

1 onion, sliced

2 garlic cloves, finely chopped

5cm piece of ginger, peeled
    and finely chopped

1 tbsp medium curry powder

1 tbsp tomato purée

4 boneless skinless chicken
    thighs, roughly chopped

1 x 400g tin chopped tomatoes

150ml reduced fat coconut milk

50g ground almonds

finely grated zest and juice
    of 1 lime

2 tbsp roughly chopped
    coriander

4 tsp flaked almonds

green salad, to serve

FOR THE ROTI (MAKES 8)

350g plain flour, plus extra
    for dusting

½ tsp sea salt

Heat a sauté pan until hot. Add the oil and onion and cook over a medium heat for 5 minutes until just softened.

Add the garlic, ginger and curry powder and cook for 2 minutes until just lightly coloured. Add the tomato purée and cook for 30 seconds.

Stir in the chicken, making sure the pieces are covered in the spice mixture, and fry for 2–3 minutes.

Add the tinned tomatoes, coconut milk and ground almonds, cover and bring to the boil. Turn the heat down and simmer for 15 minutes until the chicken is cooked through.

Meanwhile, make the roti. Tip the flour and salt into a bowl and mix together. Make a well in the centre and add 175ml water. Stir the water into the flour to form a soft dough, then tip out onto a lightly floured work surface and knead until smooth.

Divide evenly into 8 then roll each piece into a small ball. Lightly dust the work surface with flour then roll each ball into a flat disc, about 1–2mm thick.

Heat a large frying pan until hot. Add a disc of dough and cook for 1 minute on each side until just charred in places and puffed up. Set aside then repeat with the remaining dough.

Stir the lime zest and juice along with half the coriander into the curry.

Divide the curry between serving bowls, top with the flaked almonds and remaining coriander, and serve the roti and green salad alongside.

This pie is ready in the same time it takes to heat up a supermarket-bought one, and it's way healthier and cheaper too!

Super-speedy Fish Pie

600g small/medium white potatoes,
    cut into 1.5cm cubes
50g olive oil spread
1 onion, roughly chopped
1 large leek, roughly chopped
2 medium carrots, peeled and grated
50g plain flour
500ml semi-skimmed milk
1 small bunch of flat-leaf parsley,
    roughly chopped
60g 50% reduced fat matured
    Cheddar cheese, grated
500g frozen fish pie mix, defrosted
1 tbsp olive oil
½ tsp fine sea salt
freshly ground black pepper, to taste
400g frozen peas, to serve

Preheat the oven to 220°C/200°C fan/Gas 7 and put the kettle on to boil.

Tip the potatoes into a saucepan then pour enough boiling water in to just cover the potatoes. Set over a high heat and bring to the boil. Simmer for 10–12 minutes until nearly tender.

Meanwhile, make the sauce. Heat a sauté pan until medium hot. Add the olive oil spread, onion, leek and carrot and fry for 5 minutes until just softened, stirring occasionally.

Stir in the flour and cook for 1 minute, stirring constantly, until it just starts turning a light golden colour. Pour in the milk in a steady stream, stirring constantly, until you have a slightly thickened liquid.

Cook gently for 2 minutes, stirring constantly, until the liquid has thickened enough to coat the back of a spoon – draw a spoon through the sauce and lift out. Run a finger down the back of the spoon: if the sauce stays to either side, it is ready. If not, return to the heat, cook for another couple of minutes then check again.

Stir in the parsley and half the grated cheese and cook until melted, then stir in the fish pie mix and simmer for 3 minutes. Stir once more then tip into a deep-sided baking dish.

Drain the cooked potatoes and tip into a bowl. Add the oil, salt and plenty of black pepper. Mix together and pile loosely over the fish pie mix. Sprinkle the remaining grated cheese on top.

Bake in the oven for 10 minutes until the cheese is bubbling and the fish cooked through. (If the potatoes haven't browned enough, pop under a hot grill for 2–3 minutes.)

Meanwhile bring a pan of water to the boil. Add the peas and return to the simmer for 2 minutes, then drain and return to the pan.

Serve the fish pie with the peas piled alongside.

SERVES:
4
PREP TIME:
5 minutes
COOKING TIME:
20 minutes

Quick-cook Dahl

A good dahl feels like a comforting winter warmer, and this is a quick-cook one with both lentils and chickpeas, finished off with some baby spinach and it only takes about 20 minutes.

1 tbsp vegetable oil
2 tsp ground turmeric
3 tbsp curry powder
1 tbsp tomato purée
1 x 400g tin green lentils, drained and rinsed
1 x 400g tin chickpeas, drained and rinsed
1 x 400g tin chopped tomatoes
200ml reduced fat coconut milk

250g baby spinach leaves
finely grated zest and juice of 1 lime
½ tsp sea salt
2 tbsp roughly chopped coriander
freshly ground black pepper, to taste

Heat a sauté pan or saucepan until medium hot. Add the oil, turmeric and curry powder and stir-fry for 1–2 minutes until just coloured and fragrant.

Stir in the tomato purée, lentils, chickpeas, tinned tomatoes and coconut milk and bring to the boil. Turn down the heat, cover and simmer for 10 minutes until just thickened.

Pile the spinach on top of the mixture, cover and simmer for another 5 minutes until the spinach has wilted.

Stir well, then stir in the lime zest and juice, salt, coriander and black pepper.

Divide between serving plates and serve immediately.

Making your own teriyaki sauce means that you can adjust it according to your own taste – include a teaspoon of dried chilli flakes, or use less ginger, depending how fiery you like it; add a touch of sesame oil if you fancy it slightly nutty. Keep a note of what you've done so next time you make it you can recreate your favoured version.

Teriyaki Beef Stir Fry

FOR THE TERIYAKI SAUCE (MAKES 450ML)

100ml reduced-salt soy sauce
80ml date syrup
2 tbsp rice wine vinegar
3 garlic cloves, finely grated
5cm piece of ginger, peeled
and finely grated
1 tbsp cornflour

FOR THE STIR FRY

300g basmati rice, rinsed
2 tsp vegetable oil
400g stir fry beef
1 red onion, finely sliced
2 garlic cloves, finely sliced
5cm piece of ginger, peeled
and finely sliced
100ml (6–7 tbsp) homemade
Teriyaki Sauce (see above)
4 spring onions, sliced
1 red chilli, deseeded and
sliced (optional)

For the teriyaki sauce, tip the soy sauce, date syrup, vinegar, garlic and ginger into a small pan with 250ml water. Bring to the boil then simmer for 5 minutes until just reduced slightly.

Tip the cornflour into a small bowl or cup, add 2 tablespoons water and mix well. Pour the mixture into the simmering teriyaki sauce and whisk really well until smooth. Simmer for 1–2 minutes until thickened, then decant into a sealable container. Allow to cool to room temperature then transfer to the fridge where it will store for up to 2 weeks.

For the stir fry, put the rice in a large pan with 600ml water. Stir well, bring to the boil, then turn the heat down to a simmer, cover with a lid and cook for 15 minutes until the rice is tender and the water absorbed. Without stirring, turn the heat off and leave to steam with the lid on until the stir fry is ready.

160g baby corn, halved

160g green beans, halved

160g broccoli, cut into florets,
stems sliced

160g cauliflower, cut into
florets, stems sliced

2 yellow peppers, deseeded
and sliced

2 orange peppers, deseeded
and sliced

2 green peppers, deseeded
and sliced

2 small courgettes, peeled
then peeled into ribbons
with a swivel potato peeler

2 medium carrots, peeled
into ribbons with a swivel
potato peeler

160g mangetout

160g frozen peas

160g frozen sweetcorn

Prepare your chosen vegetables once the rice is cooking, so that the stir fry will be ready when the rice is ready. Don't start cooking until all the veg is chopped, and have a timer nearby; it really does help with stir fries!

Heat a large wok until hot. Add 1 teaspoon of the oil and the beef and stir-fry for 2 minutes until just browned. Tip out into a bowl and set aside.

Add the remaining oil to the wok. Add the red onion and stir-fry for 2 minutes then add the garlic and ginger and stir-fry for 1 minute.

Add the harder veg (baby corn, green beans, broccoli or cauliflower) then add 200ml water, stir well, cover with a lid and steam for 2 minutes.

Stir in the softer veg (peppers) and cook for another 2 minutes then add the quick-cook veg (courgette, carrot, mangetout, peas or sweetcorn), teriyaki sauce, cooked beef and any juices. Stir-fry for another 2 minutes until the veg is just tender and the beef cooked through.

Divide the rice between the serving plates and top with the stir fry. Scatter the spring onions and chilli, if using, over the top.

There are many ways to cook fish and chips! This one has a very light batter which just coats the fish. You need to whisk the eggs until they are really pale and thick, then whisk in the flour, keeping it as light as possible.

Home-made Fish and Chips

1 lemon
2 large potatoes, scrubbed and cut into wedges
1 tsp rapeseed oil
¼ tsp sea salt
2 eggs
2 tbsp plain flour
2 x 125g skinless white fish fillets
160g frozen peas
freshly ground black pepper, to taste

Preheat the oven to 200°C/180°C fan/Gas 6. Line 2 baking trays with baking parchment.

Finely grate the zest of the lemon into a bowl and move to one side.

Cut the zested lemon into quarters and place on one of the lined baking trays. Add the potato wedges, drizzle with the oil and season with the salt and some black pepper. Toss well to coat, then shuffle the tray around until the wedges are in a single layer.

Bake in the oven for 10 minutes while you prepare the fish.

Crack the eggs into the bowl with the lemon zest and whisk for 2–3 minutes until foamy and just thickened. Whisk in the flour, then add plenty of black pepper.

Dip the fish fillets into the batter and swirl around gently until totally coated. Transfer to the second lined tray.

Add to the oven with the chips and bake for 15 minutes until the fish is cooked through and the chips are cooked through and golden brown.

A few minutes before the fish and chips are ready, cook the peas in a pan of boiling water for 2–3 minutes until hot through. Drain and return to the pan.

Divide the fish, chips and peas between serving plates. Squeeze the roasted lemon quarters over the top of the fish.

SERVES:
4
PREP TIME:
15 minutes
COOKING TIME:
15 minutes

A calzone is simply a folded-over pizza – meaning you need to pile the toppings high on half the dough before you fold it over and crimp the edges. Use any overripe tomatoes to make the sauce, whatever vegetables you have in the bottom of the fridge for the filling, and don't forget any leftover cooked meats can go in too.

No-waste Calzone

400g self-raising flour, plus extra for dusting
2 tsp baking powder
1 tbsp olive oil
50g reduced fat mature Cheddar cheese, grated
50g reduced fat mozzarella, torn
2 tbsp roughly chopped basil leaves
freshly ground black pepper, to taste

FOR THE TOMATO SAUCE
300g ripe tomatoes, roughly chopped
1 tbsp tomato purée, or more to taste (if the tomatoes aren't very ripe or are a little watery)
½ tsp dried oregano
1 tsp caster sugar
1 garlic clove, roughly chopped

FOR THE TOPPINGS (MIX-AND-MATCH SUGGESTIONS)
2 tomatoes, sliced
2 peppers (any colour), deseeded and roughly chopped
½ red onion, finely sliced
80g mushrooms, sliced
200g leftover cooked chicken
80g drained tinned or frozen sweetcorn
1 red chilli, seeded and finely chopped, or sriracha sauce, to taste

Preheat the oven to 220°C/200°C fan/Gas 7.

Tip the flour into a bowl with the baking powder and plenty of black pepper and mix well.

Make a well in the centre and add 225ml water and the oil. Stir the liquid in, starting in the centre and working your way out so that all the flour gets added in. Pull together with your hands, then tip out onto the work surface and knead for a couple of minutes until smooth.

Lightly dust the work surface with flour, then divide the dough into 4 equal parts. Roll each piece into a ball, then flatten gently and use a rolling pin to roll each into a round, about 25cm diameter and about 3mm thick.

Transfer each round to a sheet of baking parchment (this makes it easier to transfer to the baking sheet). Set aside while you prepare the sauce and toppings.

Tip the chopped tomatoes, tomato purée, oregano, sugar and garlic into a blender and blitz until smooth.

Spoon the sauce over the dough rounds, leaving a clear border of about 1cm around the outside.

Scatter whatever fillings you fancy over half of each round, leaving half clear with just the sauce on it.

Top with the cheeses and basil then fold the tomato-sauce-covered half over the filling half. Fold the edges over to seal – a bit like a Cornish pasty.

Transfer the calzone on the parchment paper to 2 large baking trays, bake in the oven for 15 minutes until golden brown and risen, then serve.

The pesto makes more than needed for the gumbo. Transfer any extra to a sealable container and store in the fridge for up to 5 days. Alternatively, spoon into an ice-cube tray and freeze, then transfer to a sealable container for up to 1 month. Drop a spoonful into tomato soup for a little kick, or mix with some Greek yoghurt for a chunky dip.

SERVES:
4 (pesto serves 10)
PREP TIME:
5 minutes
COOKING TIME:
20 minutes

The fish pie mix here is cooked from frozen, simply poached in the gumbo while you make the pesto, which is a twist on a traditional one. Made with sunflower seeds and kale, this is great stirred through pasta or even spread on toast for a quick snack.

Fish Gumbo
with Pumpkin Seed Pesto

1 tsp olive oil

1 onion, roughly chopped

2 garlic cloves, finely grated or crushed

2 red chillies, deseeded and finely diced

1 x 400g tin chopped tomatoes

1 reduced-salt vegetable stock cube

1 x 400g tin chickpeas, drained and rinsed

1 x 400g tin red kidney beans, drained and rinsed

400g frozen mixed fish pie mix

2 tbsp roughly chopped flat-leaf parsley

FOR THE PESTO (SERVES 10)

3 tbsp sunflower seeds

2 garlic cloves, roughly chopped

75g kale, roughly chopped

40g Parmesan cheese, roughly chopped

¼ tsp dried chilli flakes

finely grated zest and juice of 1 lemon

3 tbsp olive oil

3 tbsp warm water

freshly ground black pepper, to taste

Heat a sauté pan until hot. Add the oil and onion and cook over a medium heat for 3–4 minutes until softened.

Add the garlic and chillies and cook for another minute, then add the tomatoes. Refill the empty tin with water and add to the pan, then crumble in the stock cube and stir well.

Add the chickpeas and kidney beans and bring to the boil, then turn down the heat and simmer for 5 minutes, until just reduced. Stir in the frozen fish, cover with a lid and simmer for another 5 minutes.

Meanwhile, make the pesto. Place all the ingredients in a food processor and blitz until nearly smooth, stopping and scraping the sides down occasionally.

Remove the gumbo from the heat and stir in 2 tablespoons of the pesto, then cover with a lid and leave to sit for another 2–3 minutes until the fish is cooked through.

Serve immediately, with an extra dollop of pesto on top.

Pork tenderloin is a great cut of meat – lean and tender, and cheap too. Sliced and bashed into thin slivers, the pork cooks really quickly, then rests while you cook the apples and kale in the same pan.

Honeyed Pork
with Apples

1 pork tenderloin fillet
  (about 400g)
2 garlic cloves, finely grated
  or crushed
1 tbsp finely shredded sage
  leaves
2 tsp olive oil
¼ tsp sea salt
2 tbsp clear honey
2 eating apples, cored and
  cut into wedges
4 large handfuls of kale
freshly ground black pepper,
  to taste

Cut the pork fillet in half and then cut each half lengthways so you have 4 quarters. Put into a reusable food bag with the garlic, sage and olive oil. Add the salt and plenty of black pepper, then squish together in the bag until coated in the mixture.

Flatten the pork out in the bag, then bash with a rolling pin until about 5mm thick.

Heat up a frying pan until hot, add the pork escalopes, 2 at a time if necessary, and fry on each side for 1–2 minutes until golden brown and cooked through. Transfer to a plate, drizzle with half the honey and cover with foil to rest.

While the pork is resting, add the apple wedges to the pan. Sear on each side for 1–2 minutes until just browned then add the kale with a little water, which will bring all the flavours together and steam the kale.

Once the kale has softened, add the remaining honey and toss to coat. Cook for another minute until golden brown and sticky.

Divide the kale and apples between serving plates and pile the pork alongside. Spoon the pan juices over the top and serve immediately.

While the rice cooks, prepare the rest of the ingredients then simply stir them through. Jars of roasted peppers and tins of beans are handy to keep in the store cupboard – both perfect additions to rice.

Spicy Rice *with Ham*

250g brown basmati rice, rinsed

bunch of spring onions, roughly chopped

1 reduced-salt vegetable stock cube

1 tbsp ground cumin

1 tbsp ground coriander

1 x 460g jar roasted peppers in brine, drained and roughly chopped (drained weight 360g)

1 x 400g tin mixed bean salad, drained and rinsed

250g cooked ham (see page 176), shredded

finely grated zest and juice of 2 limes

small bunch of coriander, chopped

freshly ground black pepper, to taste

Place the rice in a large pan with the spring onions, stock cube, cumin and coriander and some black pepper. Add 750ml water, stir well then bring to the boil.

Turn the heat down to a simmer, cover with a lid and cook for 20 minutes until the rice is tender and the water absorbed. Without stirring, turn the heat off and leave to steam for a few minutes.

Using a fork, fluff up the rice, then stir in the roasted peppers, beans, ham, lime zest and juice and the coriander.

Either divide between serving plates and serve immediately, or allow to cool to room temperature, then decant into a sealable container, transfer to the fridge and eat within 24 hours.

This is a fully vegetarian, gluten- and lactose-free version of the classic toad in the hole. Just as delicious as the original version, it's a perfect dish when you have a few different dietary requirements to cover.

Mini Gluten- and Lacto-free Toads in the Hole

120g gluten-free plain flour
1 tsp gluten-free baking powder
2 tsp mustard powder
2 tsp chopped fresh thyme leaves
1 tbsp onion granules
freshly ground black pepper
3 eggs
220ml unsweetened oat milk
2 tbsp vegetable oil
6 gluten- and lactose-free vegetarian
    sausages, cut in half
3 tsp vegetarian gravy granules
210ml boiling water
320g broccoli, cut into florets
320g frozen peas

Preheat the oven to 230°C/210°C fan/Gas 8.

Tip the gluten-free flour and baking powder, mustard powder, thyme, onion granules and plenty of black pepper into a large bowl and whisk to combine.

Make a well in the centre of the flour and crack the eggs into it. Add the oat milk and whisk together, starting in the middle and working out to the sides until the mixture is smooth. Set aside.

Divide the vegetable oil and sausage halves between the holes of a 12-hole deep muffin tin and place in the oven for 5 minutes. Whisk the batter once more and transfer to a jug.

Gently pull the oven shelf out of the oven and pour the batter into the muffin tin, filling about halfway up the side of each hole. Slide the shelf back into the oven and bake for 20 minutes until golden brown and risen.

While the toads in the hole bake, cook the vegetables. Bring a large pan of water to the boil. Add the broccoli and simmer for 3–4 minutes, then add the peas and return to the boil. Drain and set aside.

Serve the toads in the hole with the vegetables and a drizzle of gravy.

If you have time, cover the batter and rest it in the fridge for 1 hour – this allows the flour to properly hydrate, taking on all the liquid and will give you a slightly lighter batter.

SERVES:
4
PREP TIME:
10 minutes
COOKING TIME:
15 minutes

A twist on a classic carbonara, broccoli is added in florets, ribbons and chunks, giving lots of different textures. And then, who doesn't love a dough ball? These are super-speedy, cooking while the pasta boils, so everything is ready at the same time.

Broccoli Carbonara
with Speedy Garlic Dough Balls

300g dried spaghetti
1 head of broccoli (about 320g),
    florets and stem separated
2 eggs
125ml semi-skimmed milk
60g Parmesan cheese, finely grated
2 tbsp finely chopped chives

FOR THE GARLIC DOUGH BALLS
100g self-raising flour, plus extra
    for dusting
1 tsp onion granules
4 tbsp Greek yoghurt
4 tbsp olive oil
2 garlic cloves, finely grated
    or crushed
freshly ground black pepper,
    to taste

Preheat the oven to 200°C/180°C fan/Gas 6 and line a baking tray with greaseproof paper.

First make the dough balls. Tip the flour into a bowl, add the onion granules and plenty of black pepper and whisk to combine. Stir in the yoghurt and mix to a soft dough. Tip onto a lightly floured work surface and knead gently for a minute until smooth.

Divide the dough evenly into 8 and form into small balls, then place on the lined baking tray. Drizzle with about half of the olive oil and turn them over and around until totally coated in the oil. Bake in the oven for 10 minutes until golden and crispy.

Meanwhile, bring a large saucepan of salted water to the boil. Add the spaghetti, stir well and simmer and cook for 8 minutes.

While the spaghetti is cooking, peel the broccoli stalk into thin ribbons using a swivel potato peeler, and roughly chop the last remaining bit in the middle into chunks. Add the broccoli florets and stalk chunks to the pasta and cook for 2 minutes then stir in the ribbons and cook for another minute or so until both the spaghetti and broccoli are tender.

Drain and immediately place the colander back over the pan to catch some of the cooking water – you want about 100ml.

While the pasta is cooking, crack the eggs into a bowl, add the milk and Parmesan and whisk until smooth. Season with black pepper then set aside until the pasta is ready.

Tip the pasta back into the saucepan off the heat and add the egg mixture and half the chives. Toss really well to coat – the heat from the pasta will cook the egg so there is no need to turn the heat back on.

Tip the remaining chives into a large bowl. Add the remaining olive oil, garlic and plenty of black pepper. Add the dough balls and toss until coated in the garlicky oil.

Divide the pasta between serving bowls and serve the dough balls alongside.

weekend feasts

menu

Barbecue Chicken and Ribs
   with Sweet Potato Wedges *159*

Layered Lamb and Veg Tagine *160*

Store-cupboard Enchiladas *162*

Home-made Chicken Burgers
   (Sweet Potato Fries) *163*

Slow-cooked Fillet Steak *with Chargrilled Veg* *165*

Jamaican-style Chicken Tacos *166*

Pulled Turkey Burger
   with Crispy Sweet Potato Fries *168*

Garlic and Rosemary Chicken Kebabs
   with Salad *173*

Turkey Bolognaise *174*

Chicken and Vegetable Stir Fry *175*

Cider Braised Ham *with Bubble and Squeak* *176*

Slow Cooker Creamy Goat Curry *with Roti* *179*

Smoked Fish Burgers *with Peri Peri Chips* *180*

Thai-style Red Chicken and Veg Curry *183*

Chicken and ribs are classic BBQ dishes but don't need to be saved for the summer. Marinated in a home-made sauce, these cook in the oven but will work equally well on the barbecue come the summertime.

Barbecue Chicken and Ribs
with Sweet Potato Wedges

150ml apple juice

2 tbsp cider vinegar

2 tbsp Worcestershire sauce

2 tbsp tomato purée

1 tsp garlic granules

2 tsp smoked paprika

4 tbsp maple syrup

1kg chicken thighs, skin removed

1kg pork spare ribs

4 medium-sized sweet potatoes, scrubbed and cut into wedges

2 tsp olive oil

1 tsp dried mixed herbs

½ tsp fine sea salt

freshly ground black pepper, to taste

Put the apple juice, vinegar, Worcestershire sauce, tomato purée, garlic granules, smoked paprika and maple syrup into a large bowl or reusable food bag and mix until smooth and combined.

Add the chicken thighs and pork ribs and stir/squish around until coated in the marinade. Cover and place in the fridge to marinate for as long as you can – overnight if possible.

Preheat the oven 200°C/180°C/Gas 6 and line a deep-sided baking tray with foil.

Tip the ribs and chicken out into the tray, making sure they are all meat-/skin-side up, and pour any residual marinade over the top. Roast in the oven for 45 minutes until golden brown and tender.

At the same time, tip the sweet potatoes onto a large baking tray. Drizzle with the oil then add the dried mixed herbs, salt and black pepper and toss until totally coated. Spread out on the tray and place in the oven for about 45 minutes (depending on the size of your wedges) until golden and tender. Turn the wedges over halfway through cooking to get an even colour.

Divide half the chicken and ribs between serving plates and pile the sweet potato wedges alongside. Serve immediately. Allow the remaining chicken and ribs to cool to room temperature then transfer to a sealable container and place in the fridge. They will keep for 3 days.

The word tagine refers to the earthenware pot that this Moroccan stew is traditionally cooked in, but you don't need to have one to make this tagine. Layer the ingredients in the order they're listed so that they steam-cook all together. Using lamb leg steak means that it only needs to cook for 30 minutes.

Layered Lamb and Veg Tagine

1 tbsp olive oil

1 onion, thickly sliced

3 garlic cloves, finely grated
   or crushed

400g lamb leg steak,
   cut into 2cm dice

1½ tsp ground ginger

1½ tsp ground coriander

1½ tsp smoked paprika

1 tsp ground turmeric

1½ tsp ground cumin

½ tsp sea salt

400g white potatoes, scrubbed
   and cut into 3cm chunks

2 peppers (any colour), deseeded
   and cut into 3cm chunks

2 small or 1 medium aubergine,
   cut into 3cm chunks

½ cauliflower, cut into small florets

1 x 400g tin chopped tomatoes

1 reduced-salt chicken stock cube

120g dried apricots, halved

freshly ground black pepper,
   to taste

2 tbsp roughly chopped flat-leaf
   parsley, to serve

Preheat the oven to 210°C/190°C fan/Gas 7.

Add the oil to a casserole dish or large ovenproof saucepan. Lay the onion on top, then scatter over the garlic.

Tip the lamb into a bowl, add all the spices, salt and plenty of black pepper and mix together so the spices are evenly distributed. Tip the lamb on top of the onions in an even layer.

Layer the vegetables over this – you're creating a layered pot so that everything cooks together. Tip the tomatoes over the top then refill the tin with water and crumble the stock cube into it. Pour this over the lamb and veg, then scatter the apricots on top.

Cover with a lid and braise in the oven for 30 minutes until the meat and vegetables are tender.

Serve with the parsley sprinkled over the top.

Having a well-stocked store cupboard means you can always pull a meal together. These enchiladas serve six, but you can divide them into portions and freeze for later. Transfer to a sealable container and they will keep in the freezer for a month. Defrost overnight in the fridge then heat as needed.

Store-cupboard Enchiladas

1 tsp sunflower oil
2 onions, roughly chopped
2 peppers (any colour),
    deseeded and roughly
    chopped
1 tsp ground cinnamon
2 tsp ground coriander
1 tsp cumin seeds
¼ tsp cayenne pepper
½ tsp garlic salt
2 tbsp tomato purée
2 x 400g tins plum tomatoes
1 x 400g tin kidney beans,
    drained and rinsed
1 x 340g tin sweetcorn in water,
    drained and rinsed
1 small bunch of coriander,
    stalks and leaves separated
    and roughly chopped
6 medium wholemeal tortillas
50g reduced fat mature
    Cheddar cheese, grated
freshly ground black pepper,
    to taste

TO SERVE
3 avocados, peeled, stoned
    and roughly chopped
2 tbsp fresh lime juice
4 tbsp sour cream
2 tbsp green jalapeños
1 small bag of tortilla chips

Preheat the oven to 200°C/180°C/Gas 6 and lightly oil a large ovenproof dish.

Heat a sauté pan until medium hot. Add the oil, onions and peppers and cook over a medium heat for 5 minutes until just softened.

Stir in the ground cinnamon and coriander, the cumin seeds, cayenne and garlic salt, and stir-fry for 1 minute.

Add the tomato purée and mix well, then add the tinned tomatoes, stirring all the time. Add enough water to half fill one can, then swill the water around to get the last of the tomatoes out. Tip into the second can and repeat the swirling, then tip into the pan.

Bring to the boil, stir well, reduce the heat, cover and simmer for 10 minutes. Add the kidney beans and sweetcorn, stir well, cover and return to a simmer. Simmer for 5 minutes until all the vegetables are tender and hot through.

Stir in plenty of black pepper and the coriander stalks then set aside.

Gently fold the tortillas in half then place in the oiled ovenproof dish so they are upright next to each other. Divide the bean stew between the tortillas, then gently fold the top of each tortilla over to cover the beans. Turn them around slightly so they don't open back up.

Scatter the cheese over the top then bake in the oven for 10 minutes until golden and bubbling.

Meanwhile, make the guacamole. Tip the avocado into a bowl, add the lime juice and mash with the back of a fork until as smooth as possible. Stir in the chopped coriander leaves and plenty of black pepper, then stir once more.

Divide the enchiladas between serving plates and serve with a dollop of guacamole, sour cream, jalapeños and tortilla chips.

SERVES:
5
PREP TIME:
15 minutes + marinating
(if you have time)
COOKING TIME:
25 minutes

A take on that well-known chicken-shop burger, this chicken is really tasty with a crunchy cornflake coating. If you have an air fryer, it speeds up the cooking and gives a really crisp finish, but if not, don't worry, bake in the oven at 200°C/180°C fan/Gas 6 for 20–25 minutes until cooked through.

Home-made Chicken Burgers

250ml semi-skimmed milk
juice of 1 lemon
1½ tsp onion powder
¾ tsp dried mixed herbs
1½ tsp smoked paprika
½ tsp fine sea salt
5 boneless skinless chicken breasts,
    cut into slices 2cm thick
125g cornflakes
5 burger buns
1 large little gem lettuce, leaves
    separated
2 large tomatoes, sliced
mayo and/or tomato ketchup
    (optional)
freshly ground black pepper, to taste

Pour the milk into a large bowl, then add the lemon juice and stir until the milk looks like it has curdled – this is just turning it sour, don't worry!

Add the onion powder, dried mixed herbs, smoked paprika, salt and plenty of black pepper and mix together until combined and smooth.

Add the chicken and stir until coated, then if you have time, cover and set aside in the fridge for 15 minutes.

Tip the cornflakes into a shallow bowl and scrunch up slightly until just broken.

Lift the chicken out of the marinade a piece at a time, place in the cornflakes then toss until coated. Set aside on a plate or tray and repeat with the remaining chicken.

Heat the air fryer according to instructions, then lay the chicken in an even layer in the basket or onto the trays (depending which make of fryer you have) and set the timer for 10–15 minutes. The chicken should be cooked through, golden brown and crispy.

Lay the buns on serving plates, top the bases with lettuce, tomato and a few pieces of the chicken and a drizzle of mayo and/or ketchup, if you like, then lay the bun lid on top. Serve immediately with Sweet Potato Fries (see below).

Sweet Potato Fries

5 medium-sized sweet
    potatoes, scrubbed and cut
    lengthways into slices 1cm
    thick
2 tbsp cornflour
¼ tsp fine sea salt
2 tbsp vegetable oil
freshly ground black pepper,
    to taste

Tip the sweet potato slices into a large bowl, then add the cornflour, salt and black pepper and toss really well until totally coated.

Add the oil and massage it in so that the cornflour is coated in the oil, then place in the air fryer, in batches if necessary.

Roast for 10–15 minutes until golden, tender inside and crispy outside.

Sometimes a treat is needed, and this slow-cooked fillet steak is exactly that. Cooking the steak slowly means that it doesn't shrink, giving you a beautifully tender piece of meat. Served with chargrilled veg, this is a perfect weekend treat.

Slow-cooked Fillet Steak
with Chargrilled Veg

1 x 300g fillet steak,
    at room temperature
½ tsp sea salt
1 small bunch of asparagus,
    spears trimmed and halved
8 Tenderstem broccoli stems,
    halved
2 red onions, cut into wedges
2 peppers (any colour), deseeded
    and cut into quarters
2 tsp olive oil
80g baby spinach leaves
2 tsp balsamic vinegar
3 tbsp fresh orange juice
1 small baguette, thickly sliced
freshly ground black pepper,
    to taste

Preheat the oven to 120°C/100°C fan/Gas ½.

Season the steak with half the sea salt and plenty of black pepper then place on rack set over an oven tray.

Cook in the oven for 30 minutes – the heat is low enough that the steak will not overcook. For medium-rare, the steak should spring back when you press it gently. If not, return to the oven for another 5 minutes.

Meanwhile, heat a griddle pan until hot.

Toss the asparagus, broccoli, onions and peppers in a bowl with 1 teaspoon of the olive oil, the remaining salt and plenty of black pepper. Tip the spinach into a serving bowl.

Place the vegetables on the griddle in batches and char-grill for 2–3 minutes on each side until tender and just coloured. When cooked, add to the bowl with the spinach.

Add the vinegar and orange juice to the spinach bowl then toss all the vegetables together and set aside.

When the steak is cooked, rub all over with the remaining olive oil and place on the hot griddle for 20–30 seconds on each side, until browned. Set aside back on the rack over the tray for 2–3 minutes to rest.

Slice the steak, divide between serving plates and pile the vegetables alongside. Serve with the baguette.

Transfer any leftover vegetables to a sealable container and allow to cool to room temperature, then store in the fridge for up to 3 days. To use them in another dish, tip 160g wholewheat couscous into a heatproof bowl. Pour 200ml boiling water over the top and stir well. Cover with clingfilm and leave for 5 minutes. Fluff up the grains with a fork and stir through the cold roasted vegetables. If you fancy some spice, stir through 1 tbsp chilli sauce and 1 tbsp roughly chopped coriander.

SERVES:
5
PREP TIME:
10 minutes
COOKING TIME:
10 minutes

Jamaican jerk seasoning gives these tacos a powerful punch of flavour which is balanced with the sweetness of the pineapple and coolness of the sour cream and bean salsa.

Jamaican-style Chicken Tacos

500g boneless skinless
   chicken breasts, cut in half
   horizontally
1 x 425g tin pineapple pieces
   in fruit juice
finely grated zest and juice
   of 1 lime
2 garlic cloves, finely grated
   or crushed
2 tbsp Jamaican jerk
   seasoning
2 tsp finely chopped fresh
   thyme leaves
5 small wholemeal wraps
5 tsp reduced fat sour cream

FOR THE SALSA

1 x 400g tin black eye beans,
   drained and rinsed
1 avocado, peeled, stoned
   and roughly chopped
finely grated zest and juice
   of 1 lime
1 red chilli, deseeded and
   roughly chopped (optional)
1 tbsp olive oil
½ tsp sea salt
2 tbsp roughly chopped
   coriander
freshly ground black pepper,
   to taste

Preheat the grill to medium and line a grill tray with foil.

Place the chicken in a bowl, then strain the pineapple juice from the tin into the bowl, using the lid to retain the pineapple. Tip the pineapple pieces into a separate bowl and set aside.

Add the lime zest and juice, garlic, jerk seasoning and thyme to the chicken bowl, mix well then place the chicken on the lined grill tray.

Cook under the grill for 4–5 minutes then turn the chicken over and baste with the leftover marinade. Cook for 4–5 minutes on the other side until the chicken is slightly charred on the edges and completely cooked through.

Meanwhile, prepare the salsa. Tip the beans into the bowl with the pineapple pieces, add the avocado, lime zest and juice, chilli, if using, olive oil, salt and coriander and plenty of black pepper. Mix well then set aside.

Place the wraps on a heatproof plate, cover with kitchen paper and heat on high in the microwave for 30 seconds, or until hot.

Divide the wraps between serving plates. Slice the chicken and divide between the wraps. Top with the salsa and a dollop of sour cream and serve immediately.

If you have time, leave the chicken to marinate for 20 minutes before you start cooking.

SERVES:
3 (with leftover turkey)
PREP TIME:
20 minutes
COOKING TIME:
6–10 hours

Slow cookers are traditionally used for stews, but they work well for large joints too. Strip the turkey meat from the bones and stir back through the sauce for an easy pulled turkey. Serve any leftover meat with some steamed rice or pasta.

Pulled Turkey Burger
with Crispy Sweet Potato Fries

FOR THE TURKEY
  (MAKES 15 PORTIONS)

2 red onions, sliced

2.5kg turkey bone-in thigh joints

100g reduced-salt and -sugar
  brown sauce

50ml cider vinegar

1 tbsp sweet smoked paprika

50g clear honey

freshly ground black pepper,
  to taste

FOR THE SWEET POTATO FRIES

1 egg white

3 medium-sized sweet potatoes,
  scrubbed and cut into batons
  1cm thick

60g panko breadcrumbs

½ tsp smoked paprika

Preheat the slow cooker on the high setting, according to the manufacturer's instructions.

Tip the onions into the slow cooker, then place the turkey joints on top. Season well with black pepper.

Pour the brown sauce into a small bowl, add the vinegar, smoked paprika and honey and mix well until smooth. Pour over the turkey then cover with the lid.

Leave the setting on high or turn it down to low, then leave the turkey to cook for 6–8 hours on high, or for 8–10 hours on low.

When the turkey has 45 minutes left to cook, prepare the sweet potato fries.

Preheat the oven to 220°C/200°C fan/Gas 7 and line 1 large or 2 medium baking trays with baking parchment.

Tip the egg white into a bowl and whisk with a fork until just foamy. Toss the sweet potato batons in the egg white until coated all over.

Tip the breadcrumbs, smoked paprika and plenty of black pepper into a separate bowl and mix well. Add the sweet potato batons a few at a time and coat in the crumbs then place on the lined baking tray/s.

Bake in the oven for 20 minutes, turning the fries halfway through, until golden and tender.

3 small burger buns,
    split in half
½ Little Gem lettuce,
    leaves separated
2 medium tomatoes,
    sliced
3 gherkins, sliced

When the turkey is ready, remove from the slow cooker, discard the skin and pull out the bones. Return to the cooker and shred the meat into small strands, using a fork and spoon. Mix with the cooked onions and sauce until totally coated.

Lay the bottom half of the burger buns on serving plates. Add the lettuce and tomato, then add a generous 2 spoonfuls (about 150g) of pulled turkey on top. Top with the gherkins and the top half of the bun. Serve the fries alongside.

Decant the remaining turkey into sealable containers – you will have about 12 portions. Allow to cool to room temperature before transferring to the fridge, where it will keep for 3 days, or transfer to the freezer for up to 3 months. Defrost overnight in the fridge, transfer to a heatproof bowl, cover with kitchen paper and heat on high in the microwave for 2 minutes, then stir well.

If you have time, marinate the chicken the day before, but if not, simply thread it onto the skewers then secure with the onions on either end. The chicken is then suspended over the oven tray, allowing it to caramelise all the way round.

Garlic and Rosemary Chicken Kebabs *with Salad*

12 skinless chicken thigh
   fillets, halved
1 tbsp olive oil
1 tbsp finely chopped fresh
   rosemary
4 garlic cloves, finely
   chopped or grated
finely grated zest and juice
   of 1 lemon
½ tsp sea salt
2 onions, cut in half through
   the root, then root trimmed
   flat
freshly ground black pepper,
   to taste

FOR THE SALAD
¾ iceberg lettuce, finely
   shredded
⅓ red cabbage, finely
   shredded
2 garlic cloves, grated
180g 0% fat Greek yoghurt
6 small pitta breads
4 tomatoes, sliced
3 tbsp chilli sauce,
   or to taste (optional)

Place the chicken thighs in a bowl, add the olive oil, rosemary, garlic and lemon zest. Add the salt and plenty of black pepper and stir well. If you have time, cover and place in the fridge for up to 12 hours to marinate – if not, don't worry.

Preheat the oven to 200°C/180°C fan/Gas 6. Place 2 long wooden skewers in a container of cold water to soak (this stops them burning when you cook the chicken).

Slide each piece of chicken onto the skewers, dividing it equally between them. Transfer to a baking tray and position an onion half on either end of each skewer, so the flat root end is downwards on the tray and the cut face of the onion is towards the chicken. The kebabs will now be elevated above the tray.

Roast in the oven for 30–40 minutes until the chicken and onion are golden and cooked through.

Meanwhile, prepare the salad. Toss the lettuce and cabbage together in a bowl. When the chicken is cooked, remove the onion halves from the skewers and roughly chop, then add to the salad.

Stir the garlic into the yoghurt and season with black pepper.

Toast the pittas until hot.

To serve, divide the salad between the insides of the pittas and add the tomatoes. Cut the chicken into slices from the skewers and layer onto the salad. Add a dollop of garlic yoghurt and chilli sauce, if using, and the lemon juice sprinkled over the top.

Bolognaise is a family favourite in many households. Ring the changes and make a healthier, lighter version using turkey breast mince instead of beef, with no compromise on flavour.

Turkey Bolognaise

2 tsp olive oil
2 onions, chopped
3 medium carrots, peeled and grated
4 celery sticks, chopped
2 tsp dried oregano
3 garlic cloves, finely chopped or grated
2 tbsp tomato purée
500g turkey breast mince
2 x 400g tins chopped tomatoes
1 reduced salt chicken stock cube
½ tsp fine sea salt
375g dried spaghetti
freshly ground black pepper, to taste
5 tbsp freshly grated Parmesan cheese, to serve

Heat a large sauté pan or flameproof casserole until medium hot. Add the olive oil, onions, carrot and celery and cook over a medium heat for 5 minutes. You want them to soften but not colour – putting a lid onto the pan will help keep the moisture in and steam the vegetables at the same time.

Add the dried oregano and garlic and cook for another minute then add the tomato purée and turn the heat up. Stir well so that the tomato purée goes all through the vegetables then add the turkey mince and fry for 3–4 minutes until it is just colouring.

Tip in the tinned tomatoes then refill a can with water and add to the pan. Crumble in the stock cube, add the sea salt, stir well and bring to the boil. Turn the heat down to a gentle simmer, cover and cook for 20–25 minutes until the turkey is cooked through, the vegetables are tender and sauce reduced slightly.

When the sauce has only 15 minutes left, cook the spaghetti in a large pan of boiling, salted water for 12–15 minutes until just tender then drain, reserving some of the cooking water.

Tip the drained pasta into the sauté pan with the sauce and mix well, adding the reserved pasta water if necessary to coat all the pasta in sauce.

Divide between serving bowls and serve topped with some grated Parmesan.

If you have fussy eaters, just tip the bolognaise sauce into a blender and pulse to break down, or use a stick blender so that the mixture is slightly smoother, and the vegetables less obvious!

Stir fries always need a little bit of prep time. Make sure that you have all the vegetables prepared before you starting cooking. Colouring the chicken first of all then poaching it in with the vegetables and sauce keeps it nice and tender. You can serve this with tofu instead of chicken – simply dust in a little cornflour then fry until golden.

Chicken and Vegetable Stir Fry

180g medium egg noodles
1 tbsp sesame oil
1 tbsp vegetable oil
3 boneless skinless chicken
    breasts, cut into strips
    1cm wide
3 spring onions, finely sliced
2 garlic cloves, finely sliced
2cm piece of ginger, peeled
    and finely chopped
1 red pepper, deseeded
    and finely sliced
160g Tenderstem broccoli,
    stems and florets separated
160g baby corn
160g sugar snap peas
2 carrots, peeled then pared
    into ribbons using a swivel
    potato peeler
3 tbsp Hoisin sauce
finely grated zest and juice
    of 1 lime
2 tbsp roughly chopped
    coriander

Cook the noodles in a pan of boiling water according to the packet instructions. Drain and return to the pan with the sesame oil. Toss then set aside.

Meanwhile, heat a wok until hot. Add half the vegetable oil and the chicken, and stir-fry for a couple of minutes until coloured on the outside. Remove from the wok and set aside to keep warm.

Add the remaining vegetable oil to the wok, then the spring onions, garlic and ginger. Stir-fry for 30–45 seconds until just softened.

Add the pepper and stir-fry for 30 seconds, then stir in the broccoli and 175ml water. Cover with a lid and bring to the boil, then turn the heat down and simmer for 2 minutes.

Add the baby corn, cover again and simmer for another 1 minute.

Stir in the sugar snap peas and browned chicken and cook for 2 minutes.

Stir in the carrot ribbons and Hoisin sauce and return to a simmer – the vegetables should now all be tender and the chicken cooked through. By adding the hardest vegetables first, then the next one, they should all be tender at the same time.

Stir in the lime zest and juice and the coriander.

Divide the sesame noodles between serving bowls, then spoon the stir-fried veg and chicken over the top.

SERVES:
5 (ham serves 10)
PREP TIME:
10 minutes
COOKING TIME:
2 hours 40 minutes

A large joint of ham is a handy thing to cook every so often – it has many uses and goes with lots of things, one of which is bubble and squeak. Flake the ham into pieces and serve on top, or slice and use in sandwiches, add to a pasta salad or fry until just crispy then serve with a poached egg.

Cider Braised Ham
with Bubble and Squeak

2 onions, roughly chopped
4 carrots, peeled and
    roughly chopped
½ head of broccoli, cut into
    florets
1 tsp ground allspice
2kg unsmoked gammon joint
500ml cider
600g potatoes, peeled and
    cut into small chunks
1 tbsp vegetable oil
freshly ground black pepper,
    to taste

Preheat the oven to 180°C/160°C fan/Gas 4.

Tip the onions, carrots and broccoli into a large casserole dish, sprinkle the allspice over the top and mix well. Place the gammon on top and season well with black pepper.

Pour the cider over the gammon, then add enough water to just cover the joint.

Cover with a lid and transfer to the oven to braise for about 2½ hours until cooked through and just falling apart.

Meanwhile, get the bubble and squeak started. Tip the potatoes into a saucepan, cover with water and bring to the boil. Simmer for 10 minutes until tender, then drain and return to the pan to steam dry for a couple of minutes. Season with a little black pepper.

When the ham is cooked, remove from the casserole and set on a board. Cut off all the skin and most of the fat then transfer to a bowl. Strain the liquid over the top and set aside to cool for as long as possible.

Roughly chop the cooked vegetables so that they're all the same size.

Heat a large non-stick frying pan until hot. Add the oil, potatoes and vegetables and stir-fry until mixed. Press down lightly so that they cover the base of the pan. Fry for 2–3 minutes until just starting to crisp up at the edges, stirring so that the crispy bits are broken up, and fry for another 2–3 minutes, pressing down gently into the pan – each time you want to get as much crispy as possible. Flip over then cook the other side for 3–4 minutes until crispy. Slide out onto a plate or board and cut into 5 wedges.

Allow leftover ham to cool to room temperature, then cover and chill in the fridge for up to 3 days.

Remove the ham from its liquid and flake, using your hands or a fork, to give a pulled texture. Serve 75g per portion (about 1 small handful per serving), with the bubble and squeak.

SERVES:
5
PREP TIME:
15 minutes
COOKING TIME:
6–10 hours

Goat is becoming much more readily available, particularly online, and is a delicious low fat meat. Braised in a creamy curry sauce, it makes a great alternative to lamb or chicken.

Slow Cooker Creamy Goat Curry *with Roti*

FOR THE CURRY

1 tbsp vegetable oil

2 onions, sliced

5 garlic cloves, finely grated or crushed

6cm piece of ginger, peeled and grated or finely chopped

1 tsp ground cinnamon

3 tbsp medium curry powder

500g diced goat (a mixture of neck, breast, shoulder and leg meat)

3 peppers (any colour), deseeded and cut into chunks

200ml 0% fat Greek yoghurt

200ml reduced fat coconut milk

juice of 1 lime

25g toasted flaked almonds

2 tbsp roughly chopped coriander

FOR THE ROTI (MAKES 10)

450g plain flour, plus extra for dusting

½ tsp sea salt

½ tsp ground cumin

Preheat the slow cooker on the high setting, according to the manufacturer's instructions.

Heat a frying pan until hot. Add the oil and onions and stir well. Cover with a lid and cook over a low heat for 10 minutes, stirring occasionally, until just softened and starting to brown.

Add the garlic and ginger and cook for another 2 minutes, then add the cinnamon and curry powder and cook for another minute.

Tip the whole lot straight into the slow cooker with the goat, peppers, yoghurt, coconut milk and lime juice, stir well then cover with a lid. Leave the setting on high or turn it down to low, then leave the curry to cook for 6–8 hours on high, or 8–10 hours on low.

To make the roti dough, tip the flour, salt and cumin into a bowl, make a well in the centre and add 225ml water. Stir the water into the flour to form a soft dough, then tip out onto a lightly floured work surface and knead until smooth.

Divide the dough into 10 equal pieces then roll each piece into a small ball. Lightly dust the work surface with flour then roll each ball into a flat disc, about 1–2mm thick.

Heat a large frying pan until hot. Add a disc of dough and cook for 1 minute until just coloured and puffed up, then flip and cook on the other side for 45 seconds. Set aside then repeat with the remaining discs.

Serve the roti with the curry, with the flaked almonds and coriander sprinkled over the top.

These are made with smoked peppered herring but could easily be made with smoked mackerel if you can't find herring in the shops. Mixed with cooked spiced spelt, the texture of these burgers is light yet chewy – a delicious alternative to a classic fish burger.

Smoked Fish Burgers
with Peri Peri Chips

6 medium white potatoes, scrubbed and cut into batons 1.5cm thick

1 tbsp olive oil

2 tsp peri peri seasoning mix

250g cooked spiced spelt (see page 101)

3 x 150g smoked peppered herring fillets, skinned and pin-boned

120g drained roasted red peppers in brine, roughly chopped

½ tsp smoked paprika

2 tbsp roughly chopped flat-leaf parsley

finely grated zest and juice of 1 lemon

1 egg, beaten

2 tbsp plain flour

2 tbsp finely chopped chives

90g sour cream

freshly ground black pepper, to taste

Preheat the oven to 230°C/210°C fan/Gas 8 and line 2 large baking trays with baking parchment.

Tip the potatoes onto one of the baking trays and drizzle with 1 teaspoon of the oil. Add the peri peri seasoning and toss until coated. Bake in the oven for 15 minutes while you prepare the burgers.

Tip the spelt, herring, red peppers, smoked paprika, parsley, lemon zest and juice, egg and plenty of black pepper into a large bowl and mix it really well until combined – get your hands into the mixture and squish together so that it starts to stick together.

Divide into either 12 small balls or 6 larger ones. Flatten gently to form discs about 2cm thick, then dust on both sides with the flour.

Heat a frying pan until hot. Add the remaining olive oil and the burgers (in batches if necessary) and fry for 1 minute on each side until just golden brown. Don't fry them for any longer as they will fall apart – you just want to seal the outside crust.

Transfer the burgers to the second baking tray. Remove the tray of chips from the oven and turn them over, then add the burgers to the oven and bake both for another 10 minutes until golden brown and hot through.

Meanwhile, stir the chives into the sour cream and season with black pepper.

Serve the fries with the fishcakes and chive sour cream.

Making your own curry paste is always a great thing to do – you can then add as much or as little as you like to the sauce. Poaching the chicken and vegetables in the sauce keeps them nice and tender.

Thai-style Red Chicken and Veg Curry

1 tsp vegetable oil
1 x 400ml tin reduced fat coconut milk
1 reduced-salt vegetable stock cube
2 red peppers, deseeded and roughly chopped
200g baby corn, halved
1 courgette, thickly sliced
500g chicken breast fillet, roughly chopped
1 tbsp reduced-salt soy sauce
1 tbsp roughly chopped coriander
1 tbsp roughly chopped basil
300g rice noodles

FOR THE CURRY PASTE
3 garlic cloves, roughly chopped
3 red chillies, roughly chopped
5cm piece of ginger, peeled and roughly chopped
2 lemon grass stems, outer leaves discarded, roughly chopped
1 small red onion, roughly chopped
finely grated zest and juice of 1 lime
1 tbsp ground coriander
1 tbsp ground cumin

Tip all the curry paste ingredients into a food processor and blitz to a fine purée.

If you like a stronger curry, use all the paste, but if you like a milder curry, use only half. Transfer any you are not using to a sealable container and store in the fridge for up to 3 days, or in the freezer for 3 months.

Heat a sauté pan or saucepan until medium hot. Add the oil and curry paste and stir-fry for 1–2 minutes until just coloured and fragrant.

Add the coconut milk, then refill the tin with water and add to the pan. Crumble in the stock cube and bring to the boil, stirring occasionally until the liquid is simmering and the stock cube dissolved.

Add the peppers, baby corn and courgette and return to the boil, then turn down the heat and simmer for 5 minutes.

Add the chicken and simmer for 10 minutes until the chicken and vegetables are tender, and the curry thickened slightly.

Stir in the soy sauce and half the coriander and basil.

While the chicken is cooking, cook the noodles. Bring a pan of water to the boil, add the noodles and turn off the heat. Leave to soak for 3 minutes until just cooked through. Stir around until loose, then drain and return to the pan.

Divide the noodles between serving bowls and spoon the curry alongside. Scatter the remaining coriander and basil over the top.

sweet
&
simple

menu

Sometimes you just want a piece of cake right there and then. With this microwave mug cake, that's exactly what you get in a matter of minutes. It's lower in fat and sugar than a traditional one, but still good to have as a treat every so often.

Chocolate Mug Cake

1 level tbsp cocoa powder

2 level tbsp self-raising flour

¼ level tsp baking powder

1 tbsp maple syrup

3 tbsp semi-skimmed milk

¼ tsp vanilla extract

1 egg

5g dark chocolate (70% cocoa solids), roughly chopped

Tip the cocoa powder, flour and baking powder into a large mug and mix until combined.

Add the maple syrup, milk, vanilla extract and egg and beat with a fork; until smooth and thick.

Sprinkle the chocolate on top of the batter and stir through gently.

Place, uncovered, in the microwave and heat on high for 2 minutes then leave to sit for 30 seconds before tipping out onto a serving plate. Best eaten warm. If you like, serve with some strawberries, raspberries or blueberries.

It's quite amazing what you can do with a simple sheet of ready rolled pastry. These twists are easy and quick to make and, if you don't like raspberry, replace it with strawberry or even blackberry jam.

Chocolate and Raspberry Twists

320g lighter puff pastry
3 tbsp no added sugar raspberry jam
40g dark chocolate chunks (70% cocoa solids)

Preheat the oven to 190°C/170°C fan/Gas 5 and line a large baking sheet with baking parchment. Remove the pastry from the fridge while the oven comes to temperature.

Unroll the pastry in its parchment and place in front of you with a short side facing you (in a portrait position).

Spread the raspberry jam over the bottom half of the pastry. Sprinkle the chocolate chunks over the jam.

Fold the top half of pastry over the chocolate and jam and press down gently around the edges until sealed.

Cut in half vertically, then cut each half horizontally into 6, so you have 12 strips.

One at a time, lift each strip up and twist the ends in opposite directions to create a 'twist'. Place on the lined baking sheet, pressing each end down onto the paper to secure it – this will stop the twist unrolling.

Bake in the oven for 20 minutes until golden brown and just crisp. Remove and allow to cool slightly before serving.

These will keep in a sealed container at room temperature for 3 days or in the freezer for up to 3 months. To defrost, simply leave at room temperature for 1 hour then pop in a hot oven for 5 minutes to crisp back up.

MAKES:
24
PREP TIME:
5 minutes
+ 10 minutes soaking
COOKING TIME:
20 minutes

Dates provide both the sweetness and stickiness in these lighter-style flapjacks. You could add some grated apple and ground cinnamon for an extra flavour, or even a little mixed spice.

Peanut Butter and Date Flapjacks

200g no added salt
or sugar peanut butter
50g date syrup
200g pitted dates
300ml boiling water
1 tsp bicarbonate of soda
2 eggs
500g rolled oats

Preheat the oven to 180°C/160°C fan/Gas 4 and line a 23 x 33cm baking tray with baking parchment.

Tip the peanut butter, date syrup and dates into a bowl and pour over the boiling water. Stir well then leave to soak for 10 minutes – you want the dates to soften slightly.

Transfer the mixture to a food processor, add the bicarbonate of soda and eggs and blitz until smooth.

Tip the oats into a large bowl, add the date mixture and combine thoroughly.

Tip the mixture into the lined baking tray and press down gently until smooth. Bake in the oven for 15–20 minutes, until just golden brown, and firm to the touch.

Allow to cool in the tin before lifting out and cutting into 24 squares. Store in a sealed container for up to 1 week.

Using apple sauce in these cookies gives a nice fruity flavour, but also means that you need less fat and sugar than in traditional ones. The flour is replaced with oats and oatmeal, meaning that even though they might be small, they certainly fill you up!

Store Cupboard Cookies

oil, for greasing
125g medium oatmeal
175g porridge oats
1 tsp baking powder
1 tsp ground cinnamon
50g soft light brown sugar
50g butter, melted
150g apple sauce
2 eggs
1 tsp vanilla extract
40g dark chocolate
(70% cocoa solids),
roughly chopped

Preheat the oven to 200°C/180°C fan/Gas 6. Grease and line 2 baking sheets.

Tip the oatmeal, oats, baking powder, cinnamon and sugar into a bowl and mix well.

Make a well in the centre, then add the melted butter, apple sauce, eggs and vanilla extract and stir well until the ingredients are completely combined.

Place spoonfuls of the mixture on the baking sheets, leaving at least 2cm between each one, then flatten each to about 1.5cm thick. Bake in the oven for 12–15 minutes until golden brown and set. These are soft, chewy cookies so they won't be crispy.

Set aside to cool while you melt the chocolate, either in the microwave, or put in a heatproof bowl and set the bowl over a saucepan of simmering water, making sure the bowl doesn't touch the water. Leave to melt, then stir until smooth.

Drizzle the cookies with the melted chocolate then leave to set completely before serving. Store in an airtight container.

Yoghurt can be hard to eat when frozen on its own, but mixed with a little honey, vanilla and berries, you get a perfect lolly consistency. Add whatever berries you have to hand, or even some chopped mango or pineapple.

Frozen Yoghurt Lollies

500g 0% fat Greek yoghurt
2 tbsp clear honey
2 tsp vanilla extract
140g frozen mixed berries

Spoon the yoghurt, honey and vanilla into a large bowl and whisk until smooth. Use a large spoon to fold in the berries.

Divide the mixture evenly between 6–8 (depending on size of moulds) lolly moulds.

Insert a lolly stick into the top of each then place in the freezer for 4 hours until frozen.

To serve, dip the mould briefly in hot water to loosen, then slide the mould off the lolly.

If you don't have lolly moulds, simply line each hole in a 12-hole bun tin with a little cling film and divide the mixture between them. Freeze for 4 hours until solid, then decant and peel out of the cling film. Serve with some mixed berries.

You can use milk – oat, soy or cow – instead of water to blend the mixture.

SERVES:
4
PREP TIME:
5 minutes
CHILLING TIME:
1 hour

This dish fools people every time – the avocado flavour disappears when blitzed with date syrup, vanilla and cocoa, and you're left with a luxurious chocolate mousse. For an even richer flavour, you can use milk instead of water to blend the mousse.

Chocolate Avocado Mousse

- 4 tbsp date syrup
- 2 medium-sized ripe avocados, peeled, stoned and roughly chopped
- 2 tsp vanilla extract
- 25g cocoa powder

Tip the date syrup, avocado, vanilla, cocoa powder and 50ml water into a food processor or blender and blitz until as smooth as possible – the longer you blitz the mixture, the better mousse you'll have.

Divide evenly between serving glasses and chill for at least 1 hour until just firm.

Serve chilled.

MAKES:
30
PREP TIME:
10 minutes
+ 2 hours chilling
COOKING TIME:
2 minutes

Strawberry laces are so high in sugar, yet home-made ones are as simple as blitzing the fruit and thickening it with gelatine. You'll save yourself money and decrease your sugar intake!

Home-made Strawberry Laces

8 gelatine leaves
oil, for greasing
250g strawberries, hulled
    and washed
1 tsp vanilla extract
2 tbsp honey

Fill a small bowl with cold water and place the gelatine leaves in it to soak. Lightly oil a shallow 30 x 20cm baking tray then line with a double layer of clingfilm, making sure it comes up the sides of the tray slightly.

Tip the strawberries, vanilla extract and honey into a blender and blitz to a totally smooth purée – the longer you blitz, the better the results.

Pour the purée into a saucepan and set over a high heat. Bring to the boil, stirring constantly.

Remove from the heat and add the soaked gelatine (squeezing out all the water first). Whisk until the leaves have dissolved in the purée.

Pour the purée onto the lined tray and tap gently so that it settles evenly across the tray. Allow to cool to room temperature before transferring to the fridge for 2 hours until set.

Remove and cut widthways into strips 1cm thick. Decant into a sealable container and return to the fridge, where they will keep for up to 2 weeks.

Leave the laces to set for as long as possible to get a much firmer bite.

This bread depends on the ripeness of the bananas for its sweetness – use really overripe bananas if you like it sweet, but if you prefer your banana bread a little more savoury, then use unripe ones. Great for breakfast with a cup of coffee, but equally good as a quick dessert, served with a spoonful of Greek yoghurt and a handful of strawberries.

Banana and Chocolate Bread

125g low fat spread, plus extra
    for greasing
3 large ripe bananas, peeled
    and roughly chopped
4 tbsp date syrup
4 tbsp semi-skimmed milk
3 eggs
1 tsp vanilla extract
200g self-raising wholemeal flour
25g cocoa powder
1 tsp baking powder

Preheat the oven to 180°C/160°C fan/Gas 4. Grease a 1kg loaf tin and line with baking parchment.

Tip the all the ingredients into a food processor and blitz until smooth. Alternatively, place into a large bowl and beat with an electric whisk until smooth.

Spoon the mixture into the loaf tin and spread it out evenly.

Bake in the oven for 1¼ hours until firm to the touch and golden brown. Check that it is cooked by inserting a skewer into the centre – if it comes out sticky, return to the oven for another 5 minutes and check again until the skewer comes out clean.

Remove from the oven and allow to cool for at least 15 minutes before decanting and slicing.

Cut into slices, wrap individually then freeze for up to 1 month. Remove and place on a piece of kitchen paper on a heatproof plate. Defrost on low in the microwave for 20 seconds. If not hot, heat for another 10 seconds then check again. Repeat until hot through.

A quick store cupboard crumble, this works with whatever frozen fruit you have to hand – blueberries, blackberries, mixed berries, tropical fruit or classic rhubarb. The oaty topping makes it a much lighter dish, and also quicker to put together!

Frozen Fruit Crumble

320g frozen pineapple
320g frozen mango chunks
320g frozen pitted cherries
finely grated zest and juice
   of 2 limes
4 tbsp maple syrup
4 tbsp low fat spread
250g porridge oats
75g flaked almonds
50g mixed seeds

Preheat the oven to 190°C/170°C fan/Gas 5.

Tip the frozen fruit into a medium ovenproof dish. Add the lime zest and juice and 4 tablespoons water. Toss until coated then spread out into an even layer.

Pour the maple syrup into a bowl, add the low fat spread and mix until smooth. Add the oats, flaked almonds and seeds and stir until coated in the mixture.

Spoon over the fruit in and bake in the oven for 45 minutes until golden brown and piping hot.

Serve hot, warm or cool.

Allow to cool to room temperature then divide into portions and place in sealable containers. It will keep in the fridge for 3 days and up to 1 month in the freezer. To reheat, defrost overnight in the fridge. Alternatively, loosen the lid and place in the microwave on defrost for 5 minutes. Then heat on high for 1–2 minutes until piping hot.

The thing that takes the longest in making this quick fool is hulling the strawberries! The riper and sweeter the strawberries, the better flavour you will get, and if you like a smooth fool, blitz the strawberries for a little longer – until smooth – then add the yoghurt.

Strawberry Fool

240g (about 20) strawberries, hulled and roughly chopped
375g 0% fat Greek yoghurt
30g toasted flaked almonds

Tip the strawberries into a blender or food processor with the yoghurt and blitz briefly until just broken down.

Divide between 3 serving glasses and top the fool with the flaked almonds.

Cover and chill until needed or serve immediately.

This can be made with any berries, or even mango or pineapple – just blitz the fruit until it's properly broken down before adding the yoghurt, if the fruit is firm to start with.

Few things hit the spot more when you fancy something sweet than warm vanilla sponge with a dollop of jam. This is a lighter version of the original mug cake, ready in less than 10 minutes. If you don't eat it all, allow the sponge to cool and serve topped with no added sugar jelly, then the jam and yoghurt for a quick-style trifle.

Quick Strawberry Sponge

30g light sunflower spread
1 egg white
2 tsp vanilla extract
1 tbsp stevia
finely grated zest of ½ lemon
50g self-raising flour
1 tbsp no added sugar
   strawberry jam
2 tbsp 0% fat Greek yoghurt

Tip the spread into a medium-sized mug and heat on high in the microwave for 30 seconds, until melted.

Add the egg white and vanilla and beat with a fork until smooth.

Add the stevia, lemon zest and flour and mix until it forms a smooth batter.

Place, uncovered, into the microwave on high for 70 seconds until risen and the sponge springs back when pressed gently.

Leave for 30 seconds then spoon into 2 bowls. Top with the strawberry jam and yoghurt and eat hot.

To serve as a mini trifle-style dish, run a knife around the outside of the cooked sponge, slide out onto a plate and allow to cool to room temperature before serving with the jam and yoghurt.

Stevia is a natural sugar alternative – you can use caster or soft light brown sugar instead.

SERVES:
4
PREP TIME:
5 minutes
FREEZING TIME:
4 hours

A twist on the classic banana ice cream, the combination of peanut butter and banana gives a lovely nutty sweetness to this instant ice cream. Just remember to chop and freeze any bananas that are just that bit too ripe to eat – perfect for blitzing into an ice cream.

Peanut Butter and Banana Ice Cream

4 ripe bananas, peeled
   and chopped
4 tbsp no added sugar
   peanut butter
2 tbsp semi-skimmed milk
5g dark chocolate
   (70% cocoa solids),
   finely grated

Place the bananas chunks and place on a tray lined with baking parchment. Place in the freezer until frozen solid, about 4 hours.

Tip the frozen banana into a food processor with the peanut butter and milk and blitz until smooth; you might need to scrape the sides down occasionally.

Serve immediately, topped with the grated chocolate.

If at any time you have bananas that are in danger of becoming mushy, chop and freeze as directed, then decant into a sealable container and return to the freezer so that you have a ready supply of frozen bananas for making ice cream. The riper the banana, the sweeter the ice cream – green or unripe bananas never make a good sweet ice cream!

Cook's notes

✳ Where we've included salt and pepper for seasoning, we'd suggest using a maximum of ¼ tsp of salt for 2 servings, to make sure you're not eating too much salt.

✳ All herbs are fresh unless stated otherwise.

✳ Cheddar cheese has been used in some of the vegetarian recipes. If you're a strict vegetarian, check the packaging to make sure you're choosing a Cheddar that isn't made using rennet.

✳ All eggs are medium unless stated otherwise.

✳ We've generally used stock cubes but you can substitute these with stock pots if you prefer, which tend to be more flavourful and less salty. Also we recommend using 'reduced-salt' stock pots, if trying to lower daily salt intake.

✳ All microwave recipes in this book have been developed/ tested using a 1000W microwave oven, so if you're using a lower wattage oven, you'll need to adjust (increase) cooking times accordingly.

✳ To check that chicken is fully cooked through, firstly press it gently with a finger – it should spring back. Then, insert a knife or skewer into the fattest part of the chicken. If the juices run clear, the chicken is cooked through. If any blood comes out, cook it for another 5 minutes, then check again. Alternatively, pierce a piece of chicken with a temperature probe and check the temperature – it should be 75°C.

✳ Spoon measures are level unless stated otherwise.

- 1 teaspoon = 5ml
- 1 tablespoon = 15ml

Menu planner

Planning what you will eat over two weeks takes the strain off shopping and feeding all the family – no more last-minute panic! You'll find a great range of recipes throughout this book for switching in and out, but here we suggest a two-week plan that you can follow either as it stands or tweak to suit your needs. We have provided a shopping list for each week, plus a list of general store cupboard items to keep in stock, making things even more stress free. The list for week 1 is longer as you will handily be buying enough of some non-perishable items to use in week 2.

The menus include meat-free days and a good balance of fish, veggies and meat, with healthy carbs and delicious treats thrown in. With midweek often being busier, the weekend menus offer more leisurely and indulgent menus that you can all sit and enjoy together. There are some easy, quick desserts included, but you'll also see that some nights we suggest just fruit and yoghurt to satisfy any sweet cravings. With a ready supply of fresh, frozen and tinned (in juice) fruit, you will always have a healthy alternative to dessert.

The dishes listed feed different numbers, so check before you shop if you need to double up – remember that any leftovers can usually be frozen and reheated for a later no-effort supper, or eaten for lunch the next day. You might even want to consider some batch cooking with this in mind.

Store cupboard staples (buy every so often)

- ☐ vegetable oil
- ☐ low fat spread
- ☐ olive oil
- ☐ reduced-salt soy sauce
- ☐ reduced-salt vegetable and chicken stock cubes
- ☐ tomato purée
- ☐ reduced-salt and -sugar brown sauce
- ☐ mayo and ketchup
- ☐ onion granules
- ☐ rice wine vinegar
- ☐ bicarbonate of soda
- ☐ baking powder
- ☐ cornflour
- ☐ ground allspice
- ☐ ground nutmeg
- ☐ ground ginger
- ☐ smoked paprika
- ☐ dried chilli flakes
- ☐ dried oregano
- ☐ ground coriander
- ☐ ground cumin
- ☐ ground turmeric
- ☐ mild chilli powder
- ☐ honey
- ☐ vanilla extract

week 1

Once you have all tucked into a comforting Sunday braised ham, you will have plenty of leftover ham that can go into lunches through the week. There is also flexibility with making dishes vegetarian or vegan, or adding meat – feel free to add ham or pepperoni to the Cheat-zza, or drop the chicken in the Thai-style curry and instead double the veg or add in different veg of your choice.

Sunday's crumble will stretch to two meals, so we suggest saving the leftovers for later in the week – if there isn't quite enough, you can always slice in some extra fresh fruit, or serve with yoghurt. Making the Frozen Yoghurt Lollies this week means they will sit happily in the freezer for a ready-made dessert next week, and the flapjacks will store nicely for next week too. Finally, the Fish Gumbo will make more pesto than you need, but this can be frozen and defrosted at a later date for an instant pasta sauce.

SUNDAY

Cider Braised Ham
with Bubble and Squeak

Frozen Fruit Crumble

MONDAY

Hidden Greens Pasta (V)

Fruit and yoghurt

TUESDAY

Fish Gumbo
with Pumpkin Seed Pesto

Frozen Fruit Crumble (leftovers)

WEDNESDAY

Teriyaki Beef Stir Fry

Frozen Yoghurt Lollies

THURSDAY

Easy Margherita Cheat-zza (V)

Fruit and yoghurt

FRIDAY

Thai-style Red Chicken and Veg Curry

Peanut Butter and Date Flapjacks

SATURDAY

Fish Tacos
with Mango Salsa

Chocolate Avocado Mousse

Shopping list

Meat, poultry, fish

- ☐ 500g chicken breast fillet
- ☐ 2kg unsmoked gammon joint
- ☐ 400g stir fry beef

Veg, fruit and herbs

- ☐ 3 onions and 3 red onions
- ☐ 2 garlic bulbs
- ☐ 150g fresh ginger
- ☐ 6 red chillies
- ☐ 600g potatoes
- ☐ 6 carrots
- ☐ 2 leeks
- ☐ 300g kale
- ☐ 1 head of broccoli
- ☐ 160g cauliflower
- ☐ 2 green peppers
- ☐ 2 orange peppers
- ☐ 2 yellow peppers
- ☐ 5 red peppers
- ☐ 360g baby corn
- ☐ bunch of spring onions
- ☐ 160g green beans
- ☐ 3 courgettes
- ☐ 160g mangetout
- ☐ 2 lemon grass stems
- ☐ 2 avocados
- ☐ small bunch of flat-leaf parsley
- ☐ small bunch of basil
- ☐ small bunch of coriander
- ☐ small bunch of mint
- ☐ 4 limes
- ☐ 1 lemon
- ☐ 1 large mango

Store cupboard

- ☐ 400g tin chopped tomatoes
- ☐ 400g red kidney beans tin
- ☐ 400g tin chickpeas
- ☐ 400ml tin reduced fat coconut milk
- ☐ 375g dried pasta
- ☐ 300g rice noodles
- ☐ 300g basmati rice
- ☐ 250ml passata
- ☐ 60g pitted olives
- ☐ 375g self-raising flour
- ☐ 750g porridge oats
- ☐ 75g flaked almonds (plus 30g for week 2)
- ☐ 25g cocoa powder (plus 25g for week 2)
- ☐ 50g mixed seeds
- ☐ 3 tbsp sunflower seeds
- ☐ 75g fine polenta
- ☐ 200g no added sugar peanut butter
- ☐ 200g pitted dates
- ☐ 500ml cider
- ☐ 80ml date syrup (plus 4 tbsp for week 2)

Dairy and fridge

- ☐ 125g reduced fat mature Cheddar
- ☐ 40g Parmesan (plus 30g for week 2)
- ☐ 100g reduced fat mozzarella
- ☐ 500g 0% fat Greek yoghurt
- ☐ 300g natural yoghurt
- ☐ 2 eggs

Freezer

- ☐ 400g frozen mixed fish pie mix
- ☐ 4 x 90g frozen cod fillets
- ☐ 360g frozen peas (plus 160g for week 2)
- ☐ 160g frozen sweetcorn
- ☐ 320g frozen pineapple
- ☐ 320g frozen mango chunks
- ☐ 320g frozen pitted cherries
- ☐ 140g frozen mixed berries

Other

- ☐ 4 medium corn tortillas

week 2

This second week is even easier than week 1, as you can make the most of the lollies and flapjacks you made last week and froze. Sunday is a good day for baking, and a loaf of banana bread will see you through the whole week; freezing slices to reheat will come as a welcome end-of-week treat on Friday. So dessert this week is an instant affair, whether you go for simple fruit or these delicious alternatives.

Week 2 also offers more fabulous variety, with at least two vegetarian days and some healthy fish midweek. Calzone, like the Cheat-zza in week one, gives you plenty of flexibility with the ingredients you include, and is a good opportunity to use up any leftovers and ends of packets of veg.

SUNDAY
Honeyed Pork
with Apples

Banana and Chocolate Bread

MONDAY
Veggie BBQ Chilli
with Rice (V)

Fruit and yoghurt

TUESDAY
Turkey Bolognaise

Frozen Yoghurt Lollies (from week 1)

WEDNESDAY
Hidden Veg, Salmon and Pea Risotto

Fruit and yoghurt

THURSDAY
No Waste Calzone (optional V)

Peanut Butter and Date Flapjacks (from week 1)

FRIDAY
Layered Lamb and Veg Tagine

Banana and Chocolate Bread (leftovers)

SATURDAY
Home-made Chicken Burgers
and Sweet Potato Fries

Strawberry Fool

Shopping list

Meat, poultry, fish

- ☐ 400g pork fillet
- ☐ 500g turkey breast mince
- ☐ 200g salmon fillet
- ☐ 400g lamb leg steak
- ☐ 5 boneless skinless chicken breasts
- ☐ 200g cooked chicken (optional)

Veg, fruit and herbs

- ☐ 5 onions and 1 red onion
- ☐ 2 garlic bulbs
- ☐ 1 red chilli
- ☐ 3 carrots
- ☐ 4 celery sticks
- ☐ 400g potatoes
- ☐ 80g mushrooms
- ☐ 750g tomatoes
- ☐ 250g cauliflower
- ☐ 4 peppers (any colour)
- ☐ 2 small or 1 medium aubergine
- ☐ 1 small cauliflower
- ☐ 4 handfuls kale
- ☐ 1 Little Gem lettuce
- ☐ small bunch of sage
- ☐ small bunch of coriander
- ☐ small bunch of thyme
- ☐ small bunch of parsley
- ☐ small bunch of basil
- ☐ 2 eating apples
- ☐ 3 bananas
- ☐ 1 lemon
- ☐ 240g strawberries

Store cupboard

- ☐ 3 x 400g tins chopped tomatoes, plus 1 x 200g tin
- ☐ 400g tin adzuki beans
- ☐ 375g dried spaghetti
- ☐ 200g risotto rice
- ☐ 300g long grain rice
- ☐ 600g self-raising wholemeal flour
- ☐ 325g tin sweetcorn in water
- ☐ 200ml apple juice
- ☐ 120g dried apricots
- ☐ 125g cornflakes
- ☐ sliced green jalapeño chillies (optional)

Dairy and fridge

- ☐ 40g vegetarian hard cheese
- ☐ 50g reduced fat Cheddar
- ☐ 50g reduced fat mozzarella
- ☐ 125g low fat spread
- ☐ 300ml semi-skimmed milk
- ☐ small pot half fat sour cream
- ☐ 375g 0% fat Greek yoghurt
- ☐ 3 eggs
- ☐ 240g soya pieces

Freezer

- ☐ 80g sweetcorn (or tinned, see above)

Other

- ☐ 5 burger buns

Index

From top to bottom: the Ridewoods, the Clarkes, the Whites.

From top to bottom: the Stirrats. the Smiths, the Forsyths.

Acknowledgements

It doesn't feel that long ago that we were trying to come up with a title for a pilot episode... and now we're eight series in, and on to book number five!

All testament and thanks to an amazingly talented team who make the series from RDF West in Bristol with Fiona Gay and Kate Drysdale at the helm, hugely supported by PMs Clare King and Tasha Roche. Thank you so much. They really are a dream team and I'm very lucky to work with them all. Unfortunately, there isn't the space to namecheck everyone, but hopefully they all know how appreciated and thankful we are for their hard work and creativity. Especially in the strange times we are all living through...

And of course a big thank you to our brilliant new double act – Chris Bavin and Jordan Banjo. Your love for what you do shines through and we love working with you both.

A massive thank you to all the wonderful families who allow us into their homes and to rummage through their cupboards. We really couldn't do it without you, thank you for trusting us with your shopping!

Thank you to all the support that the BBC give us when making the series, especially our Commissioners Ricky Cooper and Nasfim Haque.

I need to say a heartfelt thank you and goodbye to our brilliant MD Jim Allen. After 12 years at RDF he is moving on. You could not wish for a better boss or supporter, he will be terribly missed.

I'd also like to thank all the friends and family of those that work on this series – the ones that have plans changed at the last minute, or have to cope with us emailing late into the night or taking never ending calls when we should be listening to you. Sorry and thank you.

To my family Rob and Matty, and Mum Carol, you support me in ways that you don't even realise. Thank you.

And finally, I'd like to dedicate this book to my wonderful Dad, Ron Scarratt who we lost in January 2021. He was a huge fan of the series and gave the best feedback – always good! We miss you.